Living With Purpose

A Guide to Clarity, Action, and Growth

By: Bridgette Gajadhar

Living With Purpose

A Guide to Clarity, Action, and Growth
by Bridgette Gajadhar

Published by Pons Veritas™
ISBN: 978-1-968471-00-2
www.ponsvertitas.com

Disclaimer

This book is for informational and personal development purposes only. The content reflects the author's experiences, insights, and perspectives and is not intended as professional, medical, psychological, financial, or legal advice. Readers are encouraged to do their own research and seek guidance from qualified professionals where necessary. The author and publisher disclaim any liability for actions taken based on the contents of this book.

For permissions, inquiries, or more information, contact: ponsveritas@gmail.com

First Edition: 2025

Table of Contents

Before We Begin: You Are Already Enough

We could start this book by talking about goals, motivation, and mindset shifts—but before anything else, let's make one thing crystal clear:

You are already enough.

Right now. Exactly as you are.

There is nothing *wrong* with you. You don't need to be "fixed." You don't need to become someone else.

This book isn't here to tell you that you're not doing enough or that you need to change who you are. It's simply here to make life easier. To help you move through the world with less stress, more confidence, and a deeper understanding of yourself and everything around you.

But none of that changes the fact that who you are right now is already amazing.

Think about everything you've already been through. The challenges you've overcome. The moments you didn't think you'd get past, but somehow, you did. You are still standing. You are still here. That means you are stronger than you think.

If you never changed a single thing about yourself, you would still be worthy of love, joy, and success.

This book isn't about changing *who you are*. It's about celebrating who you are and helping you step into an easier, more effortless way of living.

And before we go any further, let's take a second to actually appreciate you.

Self-Appreciation Exercises

Before we start setting goals, let's **pause and acknowledge everything you've already accomplished**. Growth isn't just about pushing forward—it's also about **recognizing your progress and honoring your journey**.

Take a moment for yourself right now.

Imagine This: A Conversation With Your Younger Self

Picture yourself as a child—maybe 10, maybe 15 years old. Imagine sitting across from them, looking into their eyes. Tell them about the person you've become today. Share your experiences, your resilience, your strength. What would they be proud of? What would they be amazed by? Maybe you've overcome challenges they feared they wouldn't survive. Maybe you've grown into someone they never imagined they could be. Maybe you've learned lessons that would bring them peace. You are living in the reality they once hoped for. Let that sink in.

Write This Down: A List of Wins

Grab a piece of paper or open your notes app. **Write down 5 things you've done that you're proud of.**

They don't have to be huge—just moments where you:

- Showed up for yourself.
- Learned something important.
- Overcame a challenge.

Examples:

- *"I made it through a tough time and came out stronger."*

- *"I've helped someone who needed me."*
- *"I kept going even when I wanted to give up."*
- *"I've learned how to set boundaries and protect my peace."*
- *"I've taken steps—big or small—toward a life I want."*

This is proof of your strength, resilience, and growth. Keep this list as a reminder.

Read This Again: A Reminder for When You Forget

Whenever you feel like you're **not enough**, come back to this:

- **You are already everything you need to be.**
- **You don't need fixing—you need celebrating.**

This book isn't here to change you. It's here to help you enjoy life even more. You are worthy. You are enough. You are doing better than you think. And the best part? You're only getting started.

Introduction: The Art of Living With Purpose

Life is full of **interactions**—conversations, experiences, and challenges that shape the way we see the world. Every day, we **absorb information, form opinions, and make decisions** based on what we think we know. But how often do we **stop to question if we're truly understanding—ourselves, others, or even the world around us?**

Most of us go through life **reacting.**

✓ We **listen** just enough to respond, **not enough to hear.**

✓ We **observe** just enough to judge, **not enough to understand.**

✓ We **consume knowledge** but rarely pause to ask if we're interpreting it with **clarity—or just reinforcing what we already believe.**

In a world overflowing with **voices, distractions, and information**, the ability to **slow down, listen, and gain true perspective** is more valuable than ever.

This Book Is Not a Manual—It's an Exploration

This isn't a step-by-step guide to **success** or **happiness.** Instead, it's a **journey**—one that invites you to:

✓ **Listen deeply**—because before you can understand anything, you have to truly hear it.

✓ **Ask better questions**—because the quality of your life is shaped by the quality of your curiosity.

✓ **Balance ego and perspective**—because how you see yourself determines how you navigate the world.

✓ **Separate facts from opinions**—because clarity is power.

✓ **Protect and replenish your energy**—because you can't pour from an empty cup.

✓ **Align with fulfillment, not just achievement**—because success means nothing if it doesn't feel right inside.

From Understanding Others to Understanding Yourself

We'll start with the **art of active listening**—because before you can **understand life**, you have to know how to **hear it**. From there, we'll explore how shifting **your perspective** can transform the way you approach **growth, challenges, and relationships.**

Then, the focus will shift **inward**—toward listening to **yourself,** uncovering your 'why,' and recognizing the strength in embracing your **originality**.

Because ultimately, **purpose isn't something you find—it's something you build.**

Piece by piece. Choice by choice. Thought by thought.

Shaping Your Reality with Clarity & Intention

By the time you reach the final chapter, you'll see that **understanding others and understanding yourself are not separate journeys**—they are **deeply connected.**

And once you **bridge that connection**, you'll start to see life differently.

Not as something happening to you, but as something you have the power to shape.

The Truth? You Already Have Everything You Need

This book isn't here to **change who you are**—it's here to help you **see what's already within you** and bring it to the surface with:

✓ Clarity

✓ Intention

✓ Purpose

Let's begin.

Chapter 1: The Art of Active Listening

Why Listening is More Than Hearing

Most people think listening is simply hearing someone speak. But true listening—**active listening**—goes much deeper. It's about being fully present, setting aside your own judgments, and focusing entirely on understanding what's being said, both through words and unspoken cues like tone, body language, and pauses.

Active listening is not just about absorbing information; it's about creating a safe space where people feel heard and valued. When you truly listen, you're telling someone, **"You matter. Your thoughts and feelings are important."**

The Listening Gap

The truth is, most of us aren't great listeners. Studies show that the average person remembers only 25% of what they hear. Why? Because we listen to respond, not to understand.

Here's what often happens instead of true listening:

- **We interrupt** because we think we already know the answer.
- **We assume** we understand, based on our own experiences and biases.
- **We let our minds wander** and miss the heart of what's being said.
- **We focus on problem-solving** when all someone really needs is empathy.

This creates a disconnect, not only with others but also within ourselves. When we fail to listen actively, we miss key opportunities to connect and understand.

The Power of Active Listening

Active listening is more than a skill—it's a way of being. It's about **presence, empathy, and curiosity**. It transforms relationships, builds trust, and opens doors to clarity and understanding.

In Work:

Imagine a manager who listens to their team's frustrations without interrupting or dismissing them. That manager is more likely to foster a positive and productive work environment.

Active listening also helps you uncover hidden opportunities. A client may say they want a specific solution, but when you dig deeper, you might discover they're actually looking for something entirely different than what you initially expected.

In Personal Life:

Miscommunication is one of the leading causes of conflict in relationships. By practicing active listening, you can prevent misunderstandings and create deeper emotional bonds.

For example, if your partner says, "I feel like you don't make time for me," instead of getting defensive, you might respond, "It sounds like you're feeling neglected. How can we create more time together?" or my personal favorite, "I know

I've been caught up with things and haven't given you the time you deserve, but I want you to know that from now on, you'll always be my priority".

With Yourself:

Active listening starts internally. How often do you truly listen to your own thoughts and feelings without judgment?

When you tune in to yourself, you can identify what you need—whether it's rest, creativity, or connection. This inner awareness becomes the foundation for personal growth and fulfillment.

How to Practice Active Listening

Here's how you can start mastering this skill:

Be Fully Present

Put away distractions like your phone or email. Multitasking sends a message that you're not fully engaged.

Give your undivided attention to the speaker. Notice their tone, body language, and choice of words.

Ask Clarifying Questions

Don't assume you understand everything. Instead, dig deeper with questions like:

"What do you mean by that?"

"Can you give me an example?"

"How did that make you feel?"

Asking open-ended questions invites the speaker to share more, giving you a clearer picture.

Reflect Back

Summarize or paraphrase what you've heard. This not only shows that you're paying attention but also ensures there's no miscommunication.

Examples:

"So, what I'm hearing is…"

"It sounds like you're feeling…"

Listen Without Judgment

Resist the urge to jump to conclusions or offer advice too quickly.

Sometimes, people don't need you to fix their problem—they just need to feel heard.

Practice Mindful Silence

Pauses are powerful. Instead of rushing to respond, take a moment to process what's been said. Silence creates space for deeper reflection and ensures your response is thoughtful.

The Subtle Cues of Listening

Active listening goes beyond words. Pay attention to nonverbal cues like:

Tone of voice: Are they speaking with excitement, frustration, or hesitation?

Body language: Are they crossing their arms, leaning forward, or avoiding eye contact?

Pauses: What are they not saying? Sometimes silence speaks louder than words.

Real-Life Scenarios

Here's an example of active listening in action:

Scenario 1: Workplace Conflict

A coworker says, "I feel like I'm always the last to know what's going on in meetings."

Hearing: You might respond, "Well, I don't think that's true."

Active Listening: You reflect, "It sounds like you're frustrated about communication. What could we do to make sure you feel more included?"

Scenario 2: Personal Relationship

Your partner says, "I'm so stressed about everything right now."

Hearing: You might respond, "You just need to relax."

Active Listening: You could say, "It sounds like you're overwhelmed. Do you want to talk about what's been going on?"

By choosing to listen actively, you foster understanding and build trust, whether it's in the workplace or at home.

Listening to Yourself

Active listening isn't just about others—it starts with yourself.

Pay attention to your gut instincts: When something feels off, ask yourself why.

Notice your emotions: Are you ignoring feelings of burnout or frustration?

Create space for reflection: Spend time journaling or meditating to process your thoughts.

When you truly listen to yourself, you build a foundation of self-awareness and clarity that radiates into every aspect of your life.

Reflection Exercise: Practicing Active Listening

Choose one conversation today where you'll commit to practicing active listening.

1. **Be fully present**: Remove distractions and focus entirely on the speaker.

2. **Ask clarifying questions**: Seek to understand, not respond.

3. **Reflect back**: Summarize or paraphrase what they've shared.

4. **Write about the experience afterward.**
What did you notice about the other person's response? How did it feel to truly listen without judgment or distraction?

Closing the Chapter

Active listening is the cornerstone of meaningful connection and understanding. It's not just about hearing words—it's about creating space for trust, empathy, and clarity.

When you listen actively, you:

- Deepen your relationships.
- Strengthen your inner awareness.

- Lay the foundation for personal and professional growth.

Mastering the art of active listening is the first step to living with purpose and intention. And as you continue through this book, you'll discover how listening to yourself and others is the key to unlocking your fullest potential.

Chapter 2: The Skill of Asking the Right Questions

1. Active Listening is a Learned Skill

Nobody is born an expert listener—it's a skill that takes practice and intention. At the heart of active listening is the ability to ask the right questions.

The questions you ask shape the depth of understanding you gain. They determine whether you truly see the other person's perspective or whether you rely on assumptions and surface-level information.

Think about the last deep conversation you had—what made it feel meaningful? Chances are, the person you spoke with asked thoughtful questions that made you feel heard and understood.

How the Right Questions Change Conversations

They **open the door** for deeper, more meaningful discussions.

They **show respect and curiosity**, making the other person feel valued.

They **help clarify misunderstandings** before they turn into miscommunication.

In contrast, when we ask **the wrong types of questions**, we can unintentionally:

- **Shut down the conversation** by making it feel one-sided.

- **Limit responses** to yes/no answers instead of inviting insight.
- **Project our own assumptions**, which can lead to misinterpretation.

Mastering the skill of questioning is key to unlocking a deeper understanding of others—and yourself.

2. The Danger of Assumptions

Same Words, Different Meanings

Two people can say the same thing but mean completely different things based on their emotions, experiences, or context.

Example:

Someone says, *"I'm fine."*

To one person, this could mean, *"I'm genuinely okay."*

To another, it might mean, *"I'm not okay, but I don't want to talk about it."*

If you assume you understand without asking further questions, you might miss the real meaning behind their words.

Why Assumptions Fail

- **They shut down curiosity.** If you assume you already know what someone means, you won't ask deeper questions to clarify.
- **They create emotional distance.** When people feel misunderstood, they become less likely to open up.

- **They make communication one-sided.** Instead of truly listening, you end up filtering what the person says through your own lens.

The key to breaking free from assumptions is **asking open-ended questions** that invite deeper conversations.

3. The Power of Open-Ended Questions

Why Open-Ended Questions Matter

Unlike closed questions (which limit responses to "yes" or "no"), open-ended questions:

- **Encourage deeper thinking.** They prompt the other person to share their thoughts, feelings, or experiences.
- **Show genuine interest.** The person feels heard and valued.
- **Lead to better understanding.** You get the full picture instead of a surface-level response.

Examples of Open-Ended Questions vs. Closed Questions

Closed Question	Open-Ended Question
"Did you like the meeting?"	"What did you think about the meeting?"
"Are you okay?"	"What's on your mind right now?"

"Do you agree?"   "How do you feel about this?"

See how small shifts in wording invite **more depth and openness** in responses? The goal is to make space for honest expression rather than limiting the conversation to a yes/no answer.

4. The "Who, What, When, Where, Why, and How" Framework

Great conversations are built on great questions, and some of the most powerful ones start with the **5 W's: Who, What, When, Where, and Why.** But there's one more question that adds even more depth—**"How."**

Each of these questions serves a unique purpose in shaping conversations:

Question Type	Purpose	Example
Who	Identifies key people involved and their roles in a situation. Helps shift focus from just the individual to the bigger picture.	*"Who else was involved?"* (Encourages awareness of other perspectives.)

What	Brings clarity to the situation, uncovering specific details and causes.	*"What do you think caused this situation?"* (Encourages problem-solving and reflection.)
When	Adds context by pinpointing the timing of thoughts, feelings, or events.	*"When did you start feeling this way?"* (Helps recognize patterns and triggers.)
Where	Directs attention to the setting or environment, which can influence perception and decision-making.	*"Where do you think we should focus our attention?"* (Encourages strategic thinking.)
Why	Digs into motivations, emotions, and underlying reasons behind actions or beliefs.	*"Why do you think this is important to you?"* (Helps uncover core values and priorities.)
How	Focuses on the process, action, or method behind	*"How did you come to that conclusion?"* (Encourages deeper

something, helping
to understand the
steps involved or
personal experiences.

self-reflection and
critical thinking.)

Why "How" is Just as Important

While the **5 W's** help uncover details, **"How"** adds another layer—it shifts the conversation toward **process, experience, and solutions.**

"How" focuses on action and experience. Asking *"How did that make you feel?"* opens the door for personal reflection.

"How" helps break down complex thoughts. Asking *"How do you see this situation playing out?"* gives insight into someone's reasoning.

"How" encourages growth and learning. Instead of just asking *"Why did this happen?"* asking *"How can we improve this?"* shifts the focus to solutions.

How These Questions Shape Conversations

Each question serves a different role, and knowing **when and how** to use them can completely change the direction of a conversation:

"Who" broadens the perspective by shifting focus beyond just one person. It helps explore different viewpoints and social dynamics.

"What" ensures clarity and helps avoid misunderstandings by bringing out details that might be assumed or overlooked.

"**When**" helps track emotional patterns, habits, or cycles, making it easier to understand timing and triggers.

"**Where**" can guide decision-making by considering physical, emotional, or mental spaces.

"**Why**" unlocks deep motivations, helping to uncover the *real* reason behind thoughts and actions.

"**How**" bridges the gap between thought and action, turning understanding into something practical and applicable.

Using the **5 W's + How strategically** makes conversations more engaging, helps avoid assumptions, and allows people to express themselves fully.

5. Practicing Better Questions in Real Life
Scenario 1: A Friend Feels Stuck at Work

Your friend says, *"I feel stuck at work."*

Example

Closed Question	"Do you hate your job?" (Limits response, assumes negativity.)
Open-Ended Question	"What about work feels stuck for you?" (Encourages reflection.)

Asking open-ended questions **shifts the focus to their perspective**, rather than inserting your own.

Scenario 2: A Friend Feels Overwhelmed with Responsibilities

Your friend says, *"I have too much on my plate, and I don't know how to handle it."*

Example

Closed Question	*"Are you just stressed?"* (Limits response, assumes their feeling is simple.)
Open-Ended Question	*"Why do you think it feels so overwhelming right now?"* (Encourages deeper reflection on the root cause.)

Why This Works:

The wrong approach (*"Are you just stressed?"*) makes their experience seem obvious or dismissive.

The better approach (*"Why do you think it feels so overwhelming right now?"*) helps them explore what's really causing the feeling—whether it's workload, pressure, or something else entirely.

Scenario 3: A Partner Seems Distant

Your partner says, *"I just need space."*

Example

Closed Question	*"Are you mad at me?"* (Assumes conflict and makes it about you.)
Open-Ended Question	*"I understand. Do you want me to check in later, or would you rather reach out when you're ready?"* (Respects their request while providing reassurance.)

Not Every Open-Ended Question Needs "Who, What, When, Where, Why, or How"

Many open-ended questions naturally start with *Who, What, When, Where, Why, or How*—but that doesn't mean they **have to.** Those words are simply guidelines to help you structure questions that encourage deeper responses instead of yes/no answers.

But **true open-ended questions** come in many forms. For example:

- Instead of *"Are you okay?"* (closed), you can ask *"Tell me what's on your mind."*
- Instead of *"Did you like it?"* (closed), you can ask *"Describe how that experience felt for you."*
- Instead of *"Are you mad?"* (closed), you can say *"Help me understand what's going on."*

See how these **don't** start with *Who, What, When, Where, Why,* or *How*—but still encourage thoughtful, open-ended responses?

Sometimes, No Question Is the Best Response

While open-ended questions are powerful, sometimes the most meaningful response isn't a question at all.

In this scenario, if a partner says *"I just need space,"* the most supportive response might be simply acknowledging their request:

"I understand. Take all the time you need, I'll be here when you're ready."

This allows them the space they asked for without pushing them to explain further.

The Goal: Encouraging Openness, Not Just Asking Questions

At the end of the day, the point isn't to follow a strict formula for asking open-ended questions—it's to create space for honest expression. Whether your question starts with *Who, What, When, Where, Why,* or *How,* or takes a different approach altogether, the key is to **invite deeper conversation rather than shutting it down.**

6. Listening Without Filtering

Asking better questions is only half the skill—**the other half is truly listening to the answers.**

What It Means to Listen Without Filtering

Don't prepare your next response while they're speaking. Focus fully on what they're saying.

Don't steer the conversation back to yourself. Keep the attention on their experience.

Don't assume you understand—confirm instead.

How to Confirm Understanding

Instead of assuming you "get it," paraphrase their response to check your interpretation:

"So you're saying that…"

"It sounds like you're feeling…"

"Just to make sure I understand, you mean…"

This not only shows that you're engaged, but it also gives them a chance to clarify or correct misunderstandings.

7. It's Not What You Say, But How You Say It

Words have meaning, but the way you deliver them holds power. Communication isn't just about asking the right questions—it's about *how* you ask them. Your tone, body language, and intention behind your words can completely change the way they're received.

Think about a time when someone asked you, *"Are you okay?"* in a dismissive, uninterested tone versus when someone asked it with genuine concern. The words were the same, but the feeling was completely different.

People Don't Remember What You Say—They Remember How You Make Them Feel

Conversations are more than just words exchanged—they're experiences. When someone walks away from a conversation with you, they won't remember every word you said, but they will remember how you made them *feel*. Did they feel heard, valued, and respected? Or did they feel dismissed, judged, or unheard?

The Subtleties of Tone and Delivery

The same sentence can carry different meanings depending on *how* it's said:

Neutral: "What do you mean by that?" (Curious, inviting further explanation)

Defensive: "What do you *mean* by that?" (Challenging, putting the other person on edge)

Dismissive: "What do you mean by *that*?" (Suggesting their point isn't valid or worth listening to)

A simple shift in tone can turn a question into an accusation. Being mindful of *how* you phrase things ensures that your words invite understanding instead of creating conflict.

How to Make People Feel Heard and Understood

1.   **Be Present:** Give them your full attention—no distractions, no half-listening.

2.   **Use Open Body Language:** Maintain eye contact, nod when appropriate, and avoid defensive postures (crossed arms, looking away).

3.   **Check Your Tone:** Speak with warmth and curiosity rather than judgment or assumption.

4.   **Validate Their Perspective:** Even if you don't agree, acknowledge their feelings: *"I see why that's important to you."*

5.   **Slow Down:** Rushing through words can make you seem impatient or uninterested. Pause, breathe, and let the conversation flow naturally.

Example: The Impact of How You Ask Questions

Imagine a friend is going through a tough time. Which approach do you think would make them feel more comfortable?

Wrong Approach: (Rushed, dismissive)

"You okay?" (Sounds like you're asking out of obligation rather than genuine concern.)

Better Approach: (Warm, inviting)

"You've been quiet today. What's on your mind?" (Shows you've noticed something and care to listen.)

By being intentional with how you ask and respond, you turn a simple conversation into a moment of real connection.

How You Say It Creates the Experience

The best conversations don't happen because of perfectly worded questions—they happen because of the feeling behind them. People might not always remember the words you use, but they will always remember how you made them feel. So, when you speak, don't just focus on the words—focus on *the experience you're creating with them.*

8. Reflection Exercise: Practicing Open-Ended Questions

Step 1: Reflect on a Past Conversation

Think of a recent conversation where you felt you didn't fully understand the other person's perspective.

Step 2: Identify Assumptions

- Did you assume you knew what they meant?
- Did you use closed-ended questions that limited their response?

Step 3: Rewrite Better Questions

Write down or think about **three open-ended questions** you could have asked instead.

Step 4: Apply This in Real Life

Next time you're in a similar situation, **use these questions and observe how the conversation changes.** Observe the differences in the person's body language, facial expressions and responses.

9. Closing Thoughts on Questioning

Asking the right questions is an art and a skill that strengthens connections and deepens understanding.

By replacing assumptions with **curiosity** and **open-ended questions**, you:

Allow people to **fully express themselves** without limitations.

Show genuine interest in **understanding, not just responding.**

Create a **space for meaningful conversations** that go beyond the surface.

Every time you ask the right question, you open a door into someone's world—and in the process, you become a better listener, a better communicator, and a better friend.

Final Takeaway: Ask With Intention

The next time you have a conversation, focus on **asking with intention. Instead of seeking quick answers, seek deeper understanding. Instead of assuming, get curious. Instead of asking just to respond, ask to truly listen.** The right questions don't just change conversations—they change relationships, perspectives, and even lives.

Chapter 3: The Role of Intentions in Understanding and Solving Problems

1. Solving Starts with the Right Intentions

Why Intentions Matter

When faced with a problem, the first instinct for many people is to **immediately jump into "fix it" mode.** But problem-solving isn't about being the fastest or proving yourself right—it's about **gaining clarity and understanding the situation as it truly is.**

The Best Problem-Solvers:

Approach issues with curiosity rather than assumptions.

Seek to **understand before reacting.**

Focus on **finding the best outcome for everyone involved, not just themselves.**

In contrast, when the goal is to simply **win the argument, fix things quickly, or force an outcome**, the **real** problem often gets overlooked.

The Danger of Misaligned Intentions

If your focus is on:

- **Proving you're right** instead of understanding the issue, you risk dismissing key details.
- **Fixing things quickly** instead of fully analyzing the situation, you may solve the wrong problem.

- **Controlling the outcome** instead of responding thoughtfully, you limit creativity and flexibility in finding a real solution.

Example: The Manager Who Tries to "Fix" a Conflict Too Quickly

Imagine a manager notices tension between two employees and decides to intervene. But instead of listening to both sides, they rush in and say:

- *"I don't want any drama. You both need to work this out and stop letting personal feelings affect the team."*

At first glance, it might seem like they're solving the problem, but what they've actually done is **ignore the root cause** and shut down open communication. Instead of resolving the conflict, they've **made employees feel unheard and unsupported.**

Now imagine if the manager had started with the right **intentions**:

- Asking each person **how they feel and what's been happening.**
- Encouraging **open dialogue** instead of shutting it down.
- Helping them find **a real resolution instead of forcing peace.**

The right intentions set the stage for **real problem-solving.**

2. Understanding is the Foundation of Problem-Solving

You Can't Solve What You Don't Understand

Imagine trying to fix a car engine without knowing how it works. The same goes for problem-solving: **you can't fix something you don't fully understand.**

Before attempting a solution, take the time to truly analyze the issue by asking **deep, clarifying questions** such as:

"What's really happening here?" (Instead of assuming, get the facts.)

"What are the perspectives of everyone involved?" (Listen before forming a judgment.)

"What's causing this issue beneath the surface?" (Look beyond the obvious.)

Reacting vs. Responding

The difference between a **reaction** and a **response** can determine whether a problem gets **resolved** or **worsened**.

Reacting (Impulse-Driven)	Responding (Intention-Driven)
Emotionally charged and often impulsive.	**Thoughtful and measured.**
Can escalate conflicts instead of resolving them.	Leads to better understanding and solutions.

| Based on assumptions rather than facts. | Based on listening and gathering information. |

Example: Relationship Conflict

Reacting: Your partner says they feel unheard, and you snap back, *"I listen to you all the time! You're just overreacting."*

Responding: You pause, take a breath, and say, *"I want to understand. Can you tell me more about what's making you feel that way?"*

By responding instead of reacting, you **shift from defensiveness to clarity**—creating space for real resolution.

3. You Can't Control the Problem or the Solution
Why Control is an Illusion

One of the hardest truths to accept is that you cannot control everything. Problems—whether personal, professional, or situational—often involve external factors:

- Other people's emotions, decisions, and actions
- Circumstances outside your influence
- Unpredictable events and outcomes

Trying to force an outcome only leads to frustration, unnecessary stress, and missteps. The more you try to control every variable, the more resistance you create—both in yourself and in others.

But letting go of control doesn't mean giving up. It means shifting your focus from forcing a solution to understanding the situation fully so that you can respond effectively.

What You CAN Control in Any Situation

Instead of trying to control the problem or the solution, focus on what's within your power:

Your Understanding – The way you interpret a situation directly impacts how you respond to it. Take the time to listen, observe, and gather insights before making assumptions or taking action. The more you understand, the more informed your decisions will be.

Your Approach – You always have control over how you respond. Will you react with patience and curiosity, seeking clarity before jumping to conclusions? Or will you respond with frustration and resistance, creating unnecessary tension? The approach you choose determines how others engage with you in return.

Your Intentions – Your reason for seeking a solution matters. Are you trying to fix things for your own comfort, or are you genuinely looking for understanding and resolution? Are you listening just to respond, or are you truly trying to connect with the situation at hand? Intentions shape outcomes—when you approach a problem with clarity and openness, solutions unfold naturally.

The Shift: From Control to Influence

Instead of asking, *"How can I control this situation?"* Ask, *"How can I best influence this situation for a positive outcome?"*

- You can't force someone to change their mind, but you can ask the right questions to help them see a new perspective.
- You can't make a problem disappear, but you can shift how you navigate it to find an opportunity within it.
- You can't predict every outcome, but you can be adaptable and prepared for different possibilities.

By shifting from a control mindset to an influence mindset, you remove resistance and create space for natural solutions to emerge.

The Role of Acceptance in Problem-Solving

The final key to solving problems isn't about control—it's about acceptance.

- Accepting that you can't control everything gives you clarity.
- Accepting that some things take time gives you patience.
- Accepting that the best solutions often unfold naturally helps you navigate challenges with a calm and open mind.

Ironically, when you stop trying to control everything, you actually gain more power over your life. You become more adaptable, more resilient, and more capable of handling whatever comes your way.

When you learn to go with the flow, you stop wasting energy on fighting what you can't change—and instead, you focus on moving with life in a way that works for you.

Let Go of Control, Gain Clarity

At the heart of every problem is a lesson waiting to be understood. The more you let go of the need to control, the more you'll see the bigger picture, listen with intention, and approach solutions with clarity.

Instead of fighting the current, learn how to move with it. Go with the flow. That's where true problem-solving begins.

4. Practical Example: The Power of Understanding Over Control

Scenario: A Coworker Keeps Missing Deadlines

You notice that a coworker is falling behind on their tasks, and it's affecting your team's progress. The natural instinct might be to get frustrated or assume the worst, but how you approach the situation determines whether you solve the problem—or make it worse.

The Wrong Intentions: Control Without Understanding

If you approach the situation with the intention to control rather than understand, it can lead to:

- **Assumptions** – Believing they're lazy, careless, or bad at their job without knowing the real reason.
- **Micromanagement** – Hovering over them, checking in excessively, and trying to force productivity.
- **Passive Complaints** – Talking about the issue with other coworkers instead of addressing it directly.
- **Blame Over Solutions** – Focusing on frustration rather than collaboration.

What happens when you react this way?

- They may feel defensive, unmotivated, or even resentful.
- The work environment becomes tense, making collaboration harder.
- The real issue remains unaddressed, meaning the missed deadlines will likely continue.

The Right Intentions: Curiosity and Understanding Over Judgment

Instead of jumping to conclusions, approaching with curiosity and open-mindedness leads to better conversations and real solutions.

Start with Open-Ended Questions:

Instead of accusing or assuming, try:

- *"What's been challenging for you about meeting deadlines lately?"* (Opens space for honesty.)
- *"Is there anything I can do to support you?"* (Creates a problem-solving mindset.)
- *"Are you feeling overloaded, or is there something unclear about the tasks?"* (Pinpoints potential issues.)

Consider Their Perspective:

By taking the time to listen, you might find out that they:

- Have unclear priorities from leadership – They aren't sure which tasks to focus on first.
- Are struggling with a personal issue – Something outside of work is affecting their focus.

- Feel overwhelmed – They may have too much on their plate and don't know how to ask for help.

Create a Collaborative Solution:
Once the real issue is clear, you're in a position to help, rather than control. Possible solutions might include:
- Clarifying expectations – If leadership is giving mixed signals, the team can work together to define priorities.
- Delegating differently – If they're overwhelmed, see if certain tasks can be shifted.
- Offering support instead of pressure – If personal issues are affecting their work, a little understanding can go a long way.

Why Understanding Works Better Than Control
When you shift from a control-based mindset to an understanding-based approach, you reduce resistance and increase cooperation.
Control leads to resistance.
- People shut down when they feel forced or blamed.
- The root issue remains unresolved.

Understanding leads to solutions.
- People feel supported rather than attacked.
- You create an environment where they want to improve, rather than feeling pressured.

Alternative Approach: Addressing the Issue Without Asking Questions

Sometimes, asking questions isn't even necessary—you can offer an observation instead.

"I noticed that the last few deadlines have been a struggle. I wanted to check in and see if there's anything that might help make things easier for you."

This removes blame while still addressing the issue, leaving room for them to open up on their own terms.

Control Doesn't Fix Problems—Understanding Does

At the end of the day, controlling a situation never fixes it—understanding it does. The moment you stop focusing on forcing an outcome and start focusing on why the issue exists in the first place, you're already one step closer to a real solution.

5. Responding with Understanding

Understanding is only the first step—**how you respond** to a situation determines whether that understanding leads to resolution or more tension. Responding with understanding means acting with **clarity, patience, and emotional intelligence,** rather than reacting impulsively or trying to control the outcome.

Approach the Problem As It Is, Not As You Assume It Is

Many problems become bigger than they need to be because we **react based on our emotions and assumptions** rather than seeing the situation for what it truly is.

Before responding, ask yourself:

- **"Am I seeing this situation for what it really is, or through the lens of my emotions?"**
  (*Are you responding to facts, or are your own feelings distorting the situation?*)
- **"What parts of this problem are within my control?"**
  (*Are you trying to fix something you actually have no influence over?*)
- **"How can I respond in a way that aligns with my values and goals?"**
  (*Are you reacting emotionally, or making a choice that serves a bigger purpose?*)

By taking a **step back before reacting,** you give yourself space to choose your response **instead of letting the situation control you.**

Act with Intention, Not Impulse

Once you have a clear understanding of the problem, the next step is **responding with intention rather than reaction. The Difference Between Reacting and Responding:**

- **Reacting** – Immediate, emotional, and often defensive. It's driven by impulse rather than thought.
- **Responding** – Thoughtful, measured, and based on clarity. It's an intentional choice rather than an emotional reflex.

Example:

Someone comes to you upset about something that happened at work.

- A **reaction** would be: *"You're overthinking it. Just let it go."* (*Dismissing their feelings instead of acknowledging them.*)

- A **response** would be: *"That sounds frustrating. Do you want to talk about it, or just vent?"* (*Giving them space to express themselves on their terms.*)

Responding with Understanding in Different Situations
When Someone is Emotional:

- *Wrong Response:* "You need to calm down." (*Invalidates their emotions and creates resistance.*)

- *Better Response:* "I hear you. Do you want to talk about it or just need some space?" (*Gives them control over how they want to process their feelings.*)

When a Situation Feels Out of Control:

- *Wrong Response:* "This is a disaster, everything is falling apart." (*Creates panic and stress.*)

- *Better Response:* "What's the most important thing we can focus on right now?" (*Shifts focus from chaos to problem-solving.*)

When You Disagree with Someone:

- *Wrong Response:* "That makes no sense. You're wrong." (*Shuts down the conversation and builds defensiveness.*)

- *Better Response:* "I see where you're coming from, but I have a different perspective. Can we talk about it?" (*Keeps communication open without dismissing them.*)

The Power of Creating Space Instead of Forcing Solutions

One of the biggest mistakes people make when responding to problems is **trying to fix everything immediately.**

Some problems don't need immediate solutions—they just need space to unfold.

Instead of:

- **Trying to fix someone's emotions** → *Let them process their feelings without rushing them.*
- **Jumping to advice** → *Ask if they even want advice before offering it.*
- **Pushing someone to talk** → *Let them open up in their own time.*

Respond with Clarity, Not Control

Every situation gives you a choice:

- **React emotionally** and make the problem bigger.
- **Respond with understanding** and create a space where solutions naturally emerge.

By **pausing before reacting, choosing your words carefully, and knowing when to step back,** you shift from someone who **forces outcomes** to someone who **guides conversations and decisions with clarity.**

When you lead with **understanding and intention,** you don't just solve problems—you **strengthen relationships, build trust, and navigate life with confidence.**

6. Quick Reflection Exercise: Control or Understanding?

Pick a recent challenge you faced—big or small. It could be anything:

- A disagreement with a friend or partner
- A frustrating moment at work
- Feeling stuck in a situation you couldn't change

Now, ask yourself:

Did I try to understand, or did I try to control?

If you tried to control it:

- What were you trying to force?
- How did that work out?

If you focused on understanding:

- How did that change the situation?
- Did it lead to a better outcome or at least less stress?

Redo the Scenario (Mentally!)

Imagine going back to that moment—but this time, **approach it with curiosity instead of control.**

- What open-ended question could you have asked?
- How could you have responded differently?

Now, try it in real life!

The next time you feel yourself wanting to control a situation, **pause and ask:**

"Am I trying to understand, or am I trying to control?"

If it's control—let go. Shift to **understanding,** and see what happens.

Closing Thoughts on Problem-Solving

Solving problems isn't about control—it's about **clarity.**

When you approach challenges with the **right intentions**—focusing on **understanding, listening, and responding thoughtfully**—you create space for genuine solutions to emerge.

Right Intentions = Better Understanding

Better Understanding = Smarter Solutions

True growth happens when you **let go of control, embrace clarity, and respond with intention.**

Chapter 4: The Power of Facts in a World of Opinions

1. The Only Constant is Fact

Why Facts Matter

In a world overflowing with **opinions, emotions, and biases**, facts remain the only true constant. They provide a **foundation** to understand reality, make informed decisions, and separate **truth from perception.**

Facts are objective—they remain true no matter who observes them.

Opinions are subjective—they are shaped by personal experiences, beliefs, and emotions.

Example:

- **Fact:** The Earth orbits the Sun. (*True regardless of personal belief.*)
- **Opinion:** Summer is the best season. (*Varies based on personal preference.*)

When we fail to recognize the difference, **opinions start to masquerade as facts**, and that's where problems arise.

The Power of Prioritizing Facts

When we make decisions based on **facts rather than opinions**, we gain:

- **Clarity**—We see situations for what they are, not what we assume them to be.
- **Better Decision-Making**—We make choices based on reality, not emotions.

- **Immunity to Misinformation**—We avoid manipulation and misleading narratives.

The biggest mistake people make is **treating opinions as facts**—and that's how **misunderstandings, false narratives, and poor decisions spread.**

Think about how easily misinformation circulates—**a rumor, a misinterpreted statement, or a personal belief** can be repeated so many times that people begin accepting it as truth. But **repetition doesn't make something a fact.** A belief doesn't become truth just because it's widely accepted.

This is why **learning to separate fact from opinion is one of the most powerful skills you can have.** It allows you to **think critically, ask better questions, and navigate a world full of conflicting information without getting lost in the noise.**

2. Using Knowledge to Discern Truth
The Modern Challenge: Information Overload

✓ We live in the most connected age in history—never before has information been so accessible.

✓ But with this abundance of knowledge comes a **new challenge:** How do we separate **fact from opinion?**

The Problem: The internet is a double-edged sword. While it gives us instant access to knowledge, it also creates a landscape where:

- **Opinions are often disguised as facts.**
- **Algorithms feed us information that reinforces what we already believe.**

49

- Clickbait headlines manipulate emotions rather than inform.
- Misinformation spreads faster than the truth.

Example:

Think about **social media and news platforms.** They often blur the line between **facts and interpretations**, making it difficult to tell what's objectively true.

- A post goes viral, claiming something shocking. Thousands believe it instantly.
- But was it backed by real data, or was it just someone's **opinion** presented as fact?
- Many people form **strong opinions** without ever verifying the actual facts.

How to Filter Truth from Noise

Before accepting something as true, ask yourself:

- **"Is this based on evidence or personal interpretation?"** *(Is this factually supported, or is it just someone's perspective?)*
- **"What is the source of this information?"** *(Is this coming from a reliable expert, or is it just an unverified claim?)*
- **"Does this align with other credible sources?"** *(If multiple trusted sources confirm the same thing, it's more likely to be true.)*

- **"Am I believing this just because it aligns with what I already think?"** *(Be aware of bias—truth isn't always comfortable.)*

Solution: Always **cross-reference information** from multiple credible sources before accepting it as truth.

Practical Tip:

- If a piece of information triggers **strong emotions** (anger, fear, excitement), pause before believing or sharing it.
- Reliable information stands up to scrutiny—**if it falls apart under deeper research, it's likely not the full truth.**

The key to using knowledge wisely isn't just knowing things—it's knowing how to verify them.

3. The Age of Unparalleled Knowledge

Access to Information Like Never Before

We live in a time where almost any question can be answered in seconds. Unlike past generations, where knowledge was locked away in universities, libraries, and institutions, today, the entire world's information is at our fingertips.

✓ AI, search engines, and educational platforms have made learning faster and easier than ever.

✓ The challenge is no longer finding knowledge—it's knowing what to do with it.

✓ Knowledge is no longer limited to the privileged—it's available to anyone willing to seek it.

Example:

- If you want to learn a new language, you don't need expensive classes—you can download an app, join online groups, or watch YouTube tutorials.
- If you want to start investing, expert insights, research tools, and market analysis are instantly available.
- If you don't know how to do something, you can simply look it up—there's no excuse for saying, "I don't know" anymore.

The Power of Smartphones: Knowledge in Your Pocket

We are literally walking around with **supercomputers** in our hands—our smartphones, connected to the internet, give us instant access to any information we need. The moment a question pops into our minds, we can find the answer. There's no longer a reason to stay uninformed or claim ignorance in the digital age.

Yet, with all this knowledge available, **the real skill is knowing how to use it** effectively. People learn in different ways, and once you understand how you absorb information best, you can **customize your learning experience.**

✓ **For people who love to read** → AI tools like ChatGPT, research articles, and blogs provide in-depth explanations.

✓ **For visual learners** → YouTube tutorials, online courses, and step-by-step video guides make concepts easier to grasp.

✓ **For auditory learners** → Audiobooks, podcasts, and lectures allow people to learn on the go.

✓ **For hands-on learners** → Interactive learning platforms and practice-based education provide real-time experience.

No one is saying you shouldn't scroll through TikTok or Instagram—but even those platforms have creators who make **educational and informative content** that can teach you something valuable. **Entertainment and education can coexist.**

The Role of AI and Research Tools

AI tools like ChatGPT, Google Scholar, and Coursera have transformed how we:

- Gather and analyze information.
- Compare perspectives and form educated conclusions.
- Apply knowledge to real-world decisions.

Example:

- A student in a remote village can access the same knowledge as someone attending an Ivy League university.
- A self-taught entrepreneur can learn marketing, finance, and business strategy without ever stepping foot in a classroom.

The key isn't just **having access** to information—it's knowing **how to filter, verify, and use it effectively.**

We Are Lucky—So Let's Use It Wisely

This is the **age of knowledge**, and we need to understand how **lucky** we are. Past generations had to struggle for access to information, but we have it effortlessly. Instead of taking it for granted, we should **appreciate and utilize** our resources.

The internet is the most powerful tool humanity has ever created—**what you do with it is up to you.**

4. Balancing Knowledge with Discernment
The Limits of Facts Alone

Facts are powerful—but they don't always tell the full story. Context, perspective, and critical thinking are just as important.

Example:

A statistic might state that **80% of startups fail within five years**. This is a fact. But does that mean starting a business is a bad idea? **Not necessarily.** A deeper analysis might reveal that many failed businesses **lacked proper funding or planning**— meaning those who prepare properly have a higher chance of success.

✓ **Facts are the foundation—but perspective gives them meaning.**

In today's world, people often rely on **surface-level facts** without digging deeper. The truth is, a fact on its own is just a piece of information. **What matters is how we interpret it, what context we place it in, and how we apply it to real life.** Without this, even true statements can be misleading.

Experiences as a Lens

✓ Personal experiences add depth to knowledge, but they should always be filtered through facts and logic.

Example:

A traveler leaves a bad review for a vacation destination because it rained the entire trip. Their experience was negative, but does that mean the destination itself is bad? **No.** Someone else could visit during another season and have an **amazing** time.

✓ **This highlights why we must separate facts from personal interpretation.**

Everyone views the world through the lens of their own experiences. This is natural, but it becomes dangerous when **personal perception is mistaken for universal truth.** Just because something happened to you **doesn't mean it applies to everyone.** Facts provide **a neutral baseline**, but it's up to us to **process them correctly** instead of letting emotions cloud our judgment.

Why Discernment is Crucial

Without critical thinking and discernment, people:

- Accept biased opinions as truth.
- Cherry-pick facts that support their emotions.
- Ignore broader contexts that change the meaning of information.

✓ **Better mindset:**

"Facts are neutral—it's how we interpret them that changes their meaning."

This is where **discernment** comes in. Facts don't have an agenda—they simply exist. **People, however, do.**

✓ Two people can take the same fact and use it to support completely opposite arguments.

✓ Two news sources can report on the same event but frame it in different ways.

✓ Two individuals can hear the same story and walk away with different conclusions.

This is why we must always ask:

- What's the bigger picture?
- Am I interpreting this fact accurately, or am I twisting it to fit my feelings?
- What other perspectives should I consider before forming my opinion?

✓ Discernment is about stepping back, looking at the whole picture, and making informed, rational conclusions instead of reacting emotionally.

The Balance: Knowledge + Discernment = Wisdom

We live in an age where knowledge is everywhere, but wisdom comes from knowing how to use it.

✓ Knowledge alone isn't enough—you need the ability to analyze it critically.

✓ Facts alone aren't enough—you need context, perspective, and rational thinking.

✓ Information is powerful—but only if you apply it with wisdom.

In a world where people are quick to react and form opinions based on headlines or single statistics, those who master discernment stand out.

The key is **not just to know—but to understand.**

5. Preparing Through Knowledge and Experience
Why Facts Are the First Step

✓ Before forming an opinion or making a decision, **always start with facts.**

✓ Facts provide a **solid foundation**—they keep emotions, biases, and misinformation from leading you in the wrong direction.

Example:

Someone looking to invest in **cryptocurrency** might hear a lot of hype on social media, with influencers promising quick profits. But instead of blindly following the crowd, a smart investor would:

- **Research market trends, risks, and past case studies.**
- **Understand the technology behind different cryptocurrencies.**
- **Analyze long-term sustainability instead of chasing hype.**

✓ **Better mindset:**

"I gather facts first—then I apply logic, experience, and perspective."

It's not about being overly skeptical—it's about being **informed.** Facts **reduce risk** and allow you to make decisions from a place of **knowledge, not emotion.**

Layering Experiences for Deeper Insight

✓ Once you have the facts, **layering experiences** adds depth and wisdom to your understanding.

✓ Experience helps you apply knowledge in **real-world** situations and see things from multiple angles.

Example:

A person considering moving to a new city shouldn't just rely on **statistics**—they should also consider **lived experiences.**

✓ **Fact-based research:**

Look up crime rates, job opportunities, cost of living, and housing trends.

✓ **Experience-based insights:**

Talk to locals or watch firsthand accounts from people who have lived there.

Visit the city and explore different neighborhoods to get a feel for the environment.

Read forums, blogs, and real experiences—not just government reports.

A **well-rounded decision** comes from combining both.

✓ **Facts give you a structured, logical understanding.**

✓ **Experience gives you insight into how those facts play out in real life.**

The Power of Combining Knowledge + Experience

✓ Knowledge alone **isn't enough**—without application, it's just theory.

✓ Experience alone **isn't enough**—without facts, it can be misleading or biased.

✓ **The most powerful decisions come from using both.**

   Example:

   - A doctor studies **medicine** (facts) but also relies on **years of treating patients** (experience) to make accurate diagnoses.

   - A chef learns **recipes and techniques** (facts) but masters cooking through **practice and experimentation** (experience).

   - An athlete knows the **rules and strategies** of their sport (facts) but refines their skills through **training and real competition** (experience).

✓ **Mastery comes from knowledge and experience working together.**

In a world where **people want quick answers and instant results**, those who take the time to **learn first and experience second** will always be ahead.

6. Practical Applications

Research Framework for Problem-Solving

Whenever you need to make an important decision, use this **four-step process** to ensure your choice is grounded in **logic, facts, and perspective**— not just emotions or external pressure.

a. Identify the Facts:

What are the **verified** truths about this topic?

What **credible sources** confirm them?

b. Research Diverse Perspectives:

What do **different experts or experienced people** say?
What **patterns** emerge across multiple viewpoints?

c. Analyze What Aligns with Your Situation:

Which **facts and experiences** are most relevant to your decision?
How do they **apply** to your specific goals and circumstances?

d. Make an Informed Decision:

Base your choice on **facts, perspective, and logic**—not emotion or external influence.

Example:

If someone is deciding whether to **quit their 9-to-5 job to start a business**, they can apply this framework:

a. Identify the Facts: Research statistics on entrepreneurship success rates, financial risks, and market demand.

b. Research Diverse Perspectives: Listen to entrepreneurs who have succeeded **and** those who have failed—what patterns do they share?

c. Analyze What Aligns with Your Situation: Consider personal skills, financial stability, and risk tolerance.

d. Make an Informed Decision: Weigh the **data and personal readiness** before making the final call.

Fact vs. Opinion Challenge

One of the best ways to **train your mind for critical thinking** is to **practice separating facts from opinions**. Try this challenge:

Statement 1:

Opinion: Social media is bad for mental health.

Fact: Studies show **excessive** social media use can contribute to anxiety and depression.

Statement 2:

Opinion: Electric cars are better than gas cars.

Fact: Many automakers and governments are shifting toward electric vehicles due to **sustainability concerns**.

Why This Matters:

- **Opinions** can be subjective, emotional, or influenced by bias.

- **Facts** are **neutral, verifiable, and based on data.**

By regularly practicing **fact vs. opinion analysis**, you sharpen your ability to **filter information, think critically, and make smarter decisions.**

Turning Knowledge into Action

At the end of the day, **knowledge without action is useless.** It's not enough to just gather facts—you need to know **how to apply them** to real life.

✓ **Fact-check what you read, hear, and see before accepting it as truth.**

✓ **Ask yourself: Is this factually accurate, or is it just someone's opinion?**

✓ Use the four-step research framework whenever you need to make an informed choice.

The ability to **discern truth from noise** is one of the most powerful skills you can develop in the age of information. **Master it, and you will always be in control of your decisions.**

Closing Thoughts on Facts and Opinions

✓ Facts shape reality—opinions shape perception.

✓ The most powerful thinkers are those who:

Distinguish fact from opinion instead of blindly accepting information.

Use discernment when analyzing information, questioning sources, context, and biases.

Apply facts wisely instead of emotionally, making decisions based on logic rather than impulse.

Better mindset:

"**I don't just believe—I research, verify, and think critically.**"

In today's world, where **misinformation spreads faster than truth**, mastering the ability to separate **fact from opinion** is not just a skill—it's a **superpower.**

Why This Matters More Than Ever

We live in an age where **everyone has a platform, but not everyone has expertise.** Social media, news outlets, and influencers constantly share information—but not all of it is accurate or unbiased.

✓ Opinions can be persuasive and emotional.

✓ Facts are neutral, but they require effort to verify.

✓ The ability to discern the difference keeps you from being misled.

   Example:

If a viral post claims that a certain food "causes cancer," many people will panic and avoid it without doing their own research. A critical thinker, however, will:

- **Verify the claim by checking multiple credible sources.**
- **Look for scientific studies instead of clickbait headlines.**
- **Consider the full picture instead of reacting emotionally.**

This ability to stop, think, and question is what separates those who are easily influenced from those who take control of their own understanding.

The Power of Independent Thinking

Most people react **emotionally** to information instead of **logically analyzing it**. But true power lies in **thinking for yourself**.

✓ You don't have to accept something just because it's widely believed.

✓ You don't have to follow opinions just because they sound convincing.

✓ You have the tools to verify, question, and form your own conclusions.

In a world full of noise, the ability to separate fact from opinion is one of the most valuable skills you can develop.

This mindset doesn't just make you more informed—it makes you **stronger, smarter, and more capable of navigating life with clarity.**

Knowledge is power, but wisdom is knowing how to use it.

How It All Comes Together

Being able to recognize facts is important, but the ability to apply them correctly is what makes the real difference.

That's why active listening, asking the right questions, having the right intentions, and understanding the difference between facts and opinions work together as the perfect combination.

When you listen actively, ask the right questions, and approach situations with the right intentions, facts become clearer, easier to identify, and more powerful. This combination allows you to handle any conversation, decision, or challenge—no matter who you are or where you are in the world.

Chapter 5: Balance in an Overstimulated World

1. The Overload of Modern Life
Too Much, Too Fast

We live in a time where **our minds are never truly at rest.** From the moment we wake up to the moment we sleep, we are surrounded by a constant flow of information. Social media, news updates, group chats, and emails make it feel like we are always **on call**—like we are expected to respond, absorb, and react to everything, all at once.

The pressure to:

- **Know more** (stay informed, keep up with the latest trends, learn new skills).
- **Do more** (hustle, work longer hours, be productive at all times).
- **Be more** (improve ourselves, look better, achieve more, fit into societal expectations).

... creates a **never-ending cycle of overstimulation** that leaves people feeling anxious, exhausted, and disconnected from themselves.

Instead of truly experiencing life, many people are simply **reacting to it**—always responding to notifications, filling every moment with distractions, and **losing their ability to just be.**

The Cost of Overstimulation

Overstimulation isn't just a mental burden—it affects **every part of our well-being**:

Mental Fatigue

- The brain wasn't designed to process constant input without rest.
- Decision fatigue sets in—leading to **indecisiveness, forgetfulness, and lack of clarity.**

Emotional Burnout
- Being exposed to **too many opinions, too much negativity, and endless comparison** is emotionally draining.
- People start feeling like they're **not good enough** because they're always measuring themselves against unrealistic standards.

Physical Stress
- **Too much screen time, lack of deep sleep, and overexposure to digital stimulation** keep the nervous system in a **constant state of alertness.**
- This leads to **poor sleep quality, increased anxiety, and chronic exhaustion.**

If we **never slow down**, we risk becoming **numb to our own lives**—always chasing something but never feeling truly present.

2. Finding Balance Amid the Noise

Why Balance Matters

Balance isn't about completely cutting off stimulation—it's about learning how to filter what's necessary and eliminate the excess. We live in a world where information is constant, notifications are endless, and distractions are everywhere. If we don't manage what we consume, our minds become cluttered with noise, making it difficult to focus on what truly matters.

Think of your mind as a cup.

✓ When it's filled with too much noise, there's no space for what's important.

✓ When you intentionally choose what to consume, you create room for clarity, creativity, and peace.

When your life is balanced, you:

✓ Think clearly instead of feeling overwhelmed.

✓ Feel emotionally stable instead of reactive.

✓ Have energy for what actually fulfills you.

The Power of Intentional Consumption

Every single piece of content you consume affects you, whether you realize it or not. The music you listen to, the social media posts you scroll through, the conversations you engage in—it all shapes your thoughts, emotions, and mindset.

Example:

Two people spend an hour on their phones, but their experiences leave them feeling completely different.

- **Person A**: Spends an hour doom-scrolling, reading toxic news, and engaging in negative social media debates. They close their phone feeling drained, anxious, and frustrated.

- **Person B**: Spends an hour reading inspiring content, listening to an uplifting podcast, or learning a new skill. They close their phone feeling energized, motivated, and mentally refreshed.

Same amount of time spent, two completely different results.

✓ It's not about cutting off technology—it's about using it wisely.

✓ It's not about avoiding media—it's about choosing what actually benefits you.

Balance isn't just about reducing input—it's about being intentional with what you allow in.

Creating Space for What Matters

To truly find balance, you must ask yourself:

- Is what I'm consuming adding value to my life?
- Does this content drain me, or does it empower me?
- Am I using my time wisely, or am I just mindlessly consuming?

✓ When you limit distractions, you make space for deeper thinking.

✓ When you filter out negativity, you allow room for peace and joy.

✓ When you stop overstimulating your mind, creativity flows naturally.

At the end of the day, balance isn't just about what you remove—it's about what you replace it with.

Less noise, more clarity. Less distraction, more fulfillment. Less overwhelm, more peace.

3. Practical Strategies for Balance

Unplug Regularly

- Your brain needs **downtime** to process information and reset.

Schedule "No-Phone" Time

- Set specific times each day when you **intentionally disconnect** from digital distractions.

- Example: **A no-phone hour before bed** to allow your mind to unwind.
- Use **app blockers** to limit unnecessary scrolling.

Create a Wind-Down Routine
- Swap **screens for books, journaling, or meditation** at night.
- Reduce **blue light exposure** at least 1 hour before sleep.

Real-Life Shift: Many high-performing individuals **disconnect before bed** to clear their minds and enhance creativity.

Set Boundaries for Input
- **Not all information is valuable or necessary.**

Limit the Number of Voices You Listen To
- Be **selective** about who and what you give your attention to.
- Follow fewer **accounts, unsubscribe from unnecessary emails, and mute distractions.**

Stop Absorbing Unnecessary Opinions
- **You don't need 10 different opinions on every topic.**
- Avoid **doomscrolling**—which is consuming **negative content excessively** without taking action.

Ask Yourself Before Consuming:
- "Do I really need this information right now?"
- "Will this benefit my mental and emotional well-being?"

Example: Instead of reading a hundred conflicting opinions on a news topic, read **one or two credible sources**, then move on.

Prioritize Rest and Recovery

Why? Rest is **non-negotiable** for a healthy mind and body.

✓ **Respect Natural Sleep Rhythms**

- Aim for **7-9 hours of sleep** per night.
- Sleep between **10 p.m. and 2 a.m.** is the most restorative.

Rest Beyond Sleep

- Stillness isn't **unproductive**—it's a necessity.
- Take **slow mornings** instead of jumping straight into digital distractions.

Example: Many **highly creative people** schedule **thinking time** to allow their minds to process without distractions.

Practice Mindful Consumption

Why? We consume more than food—we consume **thoughts, media, and energy.**

Before consuming any content, ask:

"Is this adding value to my life?"

"Will this uplift me or drain me?"

Swap Mindless Consumption for Intentional Learning

- Instead of scrolling **endless videos**, listen to **audiobooks or engaging discussions.**
- Engage in **deep reading instead of shallow headlines.**

Daily Centering Practices

Why? A daily reset helps **clear mental clutter.**

    ✓ **5-Minute Reset Ideas:**

- **Deep breathing exercises.**
- **Gratitude journaling.**
- **Taking a silent walk.**

Even a **few mindful minutes a day** can create a sense of balance.

4. Balancing Input with Output

Create More Than You Consume

Why? Too much input without output leads to stagnation—and in some cases, even depression. When you're constantly consuming information without applying it, your mind becomes overloaded, and your sense of progress feels stuck.

Shift from Consumer to Creator

Instead of watching others create, make something yourself. Instead of consuming fitness content, get up and exercise. Instead of endlessly reading about success stories, take the first step toward your own goals.

Protect Your Energy for Meaningful Work

Balance entertainment with productivity so you're not just absorbing—you're contributing. Dedicate time to hobbies, creative expression, or passion projects that bring you joy and fulfillment.

    Example:

Successful writers limit their internet time to stay focused on writing. Instead of getting lost in distractions, they protect their energy for what truly matters—creating something of value.

The Fulfillment of Purposeful Action
Why? True balance comes from taking action instead of just absorbing. Knowledge is powerful, but if you never apply it, it remains unused potential.

Shift from Reacting to Responding
Instead of being consumed by external noise, focus on your internal goals. Instead of constantly reacting to what you see, hear, or read—start doing. Spend time doing, not just observing. Reading about success won't make you successful. Watching people work out won't get you in shape. Seeing others build businesses won't make you an entrepreneur. It's not just about what you consume—it's about what you create.

The Balance Between Learning and Action
Knowledge is important—but execution is everything. Consuming information is helpful—but applying it is transformational. Observing can be inspiring—but creating is fulfilling. At the end of the day, life isn't meant to be lived through a screen—it's meant to be experienced firsthand. The shift from consumer to creator is the key to unlocking your full potential.

5. Reflection Exercise: Designing Your Balance
Finding balance isn't about removing everything—it's about **intentionally designing a life that prioritizes clarity, focus, and**

well-being. This exercise will help you identify where your energy is going and how to shift toward a **healthier, more balanced** state of mind.

a. Identify Overstimulation

Why? You can't fix what you don't acknowledge. The first step is recognizing **what's draining your mental energy.**

✓ Write down **three major sources of overwhelm** in your daily life.

Common sources include:

- **Social media overload** – Doomscrolling, constant notifications, comparison traps.
- **Work stress** – High expectations, multitasking, pressure to always be 'on.'
- **Too many commitments** – Saying yes to everything, feeling stretched thin.
- **Information overload** – Consuming too much content without application.

Example:

- "I feel exhausted after scrolling social media for hours."
- "My work schedule leaves me no time for personal projects."
- "I'm constantly multitasking, and it's making me feel scattered."

Awareness is the first step to change. Once you see where your energy is being drained, you can take action to fix it.

b. Reduce Excess Noise

Why? Cutting out **unnecessary input** helps create space for what truly matters. Instead of passively letting distractions take over, choose **one action to reduce the excess noise.**

Pick one habit to **limit distractions and regain control.**

- **Limit scrolling** – Set time boundaries for social media (e.g., no phone before bed).
- **Mute notifications** – Turn off non-essential alerts to avoid constant interruptions.
- **Declutter your digital space** – Unfollow negative accounts, unsubscribe from emails.
- **Set a 'quiet time'** – A specific part of the day where you disconnect.

Example:

- "I will turn off notifications for non-essential apps."
- "I will limit my social media use to 30 minutes a day."
- "I will take a break from multitasking and focus on **one** thing at a time."

✓ It's not about eliminating everything—it's about reducing what doesn't serve you.

c. Reconnect with Yourself

Why? Once you reduce excess noise, you need to **fill that space with something grounding.** Creating habits that **center you** will help restore balance and peace of mind.

✓ Choose **one grounding habit** to do daily.

- **Journaling** – Write down your thoughts, reflect on your day, or set intentions.

- **Walking in nature** – Get fresh air, clear your mind, and reset your energy.
- **Silence & stillness** – Practice meditation, deep breathing, or quiet time.
- **Creative expression** – Draw, write, play music—something that fuels your soul.

Example:

- "Every morning, I will journal for 5 minutes before checking my phone."
- "I will take a 10-minute walk after work to clear my mind."
- "I will have 15 minutes of quiet time before bed—no screens, just stillness."

✓ **The goal is to replace overstimulation with habits that recharge you.**

Taking Control of Your Life

Balance isn't about **perfection**—it's about **intention**. It's not about eliminating everything that stimulates or distracts you, but about **choosing what deserves your energy** and what doesn't. Every day, you are presented with endless information, opinions, and influences. The key to true balance is learning to **filter out the noise so you can focus on what truly fulfills you.**

When you:

✓ **Reduce external noise**, limiting distractions that drain you.

✓ **Prioritize your energy and time**, being mindful of where you invest yourself.

✓ **Make space for what truly matters**, ensuring that your mind isn't cluttered with excess.

...you regain control over your **mind, emotions, and life.**

Balance is about **alignment.** It's about making sure your actions, thoughts, and priorities reflect what actually serves your growth, peace, and happiness. You don't have to be perfect. You don't have to do everything at once. You just have to be **intentional.**

At the end of the day, **your time, your attention, and your energy are yours to manage.** When you choose wisely, you create a life that feels **clear, peaceful, and fulfilling.**

Less noise. More clarity. More YOU.

Chapter 6: Pouring Into Your Own Cup – The Art of Replenishment

1. Why Pouring Into Yourself is Different from Self-Care

Self-Care vs. Replenishment

A lot of people think taking care of themselves simply means practicing **self-care**—getting enough sleep, eating well, or taking a day off when needed. While these things are essential, **true replenishment goes deeper.**

✓ **Self-care is about maintenance.** It's making sure your basic needs are met—resting when tired, eating nutritious meals, and staying hydrated. It helps you avoid burnout and keeps you functioning.

✓ **Pouring into yourself is about fulfillment.** It's not just about survival; it's about **thriving.** It's about **doing things that bring you joy, inspiration, and renewed energy.**

Example:

- **A bubble bath** might help you relax after a long day (**self-care**).
- **Painting, writing, traveling, or learning something new** reignites passion and excitement (**replenishment**).

Think of self-care as keeping your body and mind in balance, while pouring into your cup is about nourishing your soul.

✓ **One keeps you from running on empty, while the other fills you up.**

Without self-care, you burn out. Without replenishment, you **lose your spark. You need both.**

2. The Dangers of an Empty Cup

When You're Running on Empty

Giving to others without replenishing yourself leads to **burnout, frustration, and emotional depletion.** Many people push through exhaustion, ignoring the warning signs until they **hit a breaking point.**

Signs Your Cup is Empty:

- **You feel exhausted even after resting.** Your body might be getting sleep, but your soul isn't getting fulfillment. You wake up just as drained as when you went to bed.

- **You start to resent the people or tasks you're giving your energy to.** Instead of helping out of love, you feel obligated and depleted. Tasks that once felt rewarding now feel like burdens.

- **You lose interest in things that once brought you joy.** When you're constantly giving without refilling, your passions, creativity, and excitement for life fade.

Many people **ignore these signs,** believing they just need to push harder or that taking time for themselves is selfish. But the truth is, **you can't pour from an empty cup.**

Why It's Not Selfish to Focus on Yourself

Society often **romanticizes self-sacrifice,** making people believe that being a "good person" means always putting others first. But constantly **depleting yourself doesn't make you selfless—it makes you unsustainable.**

When your needs are met, you:

✓ Show up better in your **relationships, work, and personal life.**

✓ Give from a place of **love, not obligation.**

✓ Become **more patient, present, and joyful.**

Example:

A parent who **never takes a break** for themselves may become **irritable and short-tempered,** making them less effective in their role. But a parent who **takes time to recharge** can be **more present, patient, and emotionally available** for their child.

The same applies to **work, friendships, and any area of life.** If you're constantly overextended, your performance and relationships suffer. But when you **take care of yourself,** everyone around you benefits too.

Taking care of yourself isn't selfish—it's necessary. The better you treat yourself, the better you can show up for others.

Your well-being isn't a luxury—it's a requirement.

3. The Dangers of an Overflowing Cup
Why Overfilling Isn't Balance

While it's important to pour into yourself, **there's a difference between fulfillment and self-absorption.** When you focus too much on yourself without considering others, you risk creating emotional distance in your relationships.

Self-care and personal growth are essential, but when they become excessive—when everything revolves around your own needs, wants, and goals—you may unintentionally **disconnect from the people who matter most.**

The goal isn't to **hoard energy** for yourself. It's to maintain a **healthy, flowing balance** where you are fulfilled **without becoming closed off** from the world around you.

Example:

- Someone who spends all their time **chasing personal success** without making time for loved ones may find themselves successful—but lonely.

- Someone who prioritizes their needs **while still nurturing relationships** creates a life filled with both **fulfillment and connection.**

It's not about choosing between **yourself or others**—it's about making sure **both coexist in harmony.**

Balance is the Key

A **balanced cup** means:

✓ Enough for yourself.

✓ Enough to share.

✓ Not so much that it becomes excessive or stagnant.

When you overfill your cup without ever sharing, that energy has **nowhere to go.** Just like water that sits still for too long, it can become **stale and isolating.**

On the other hand, constantly **giving without refilling** leads to **exhaustion and resentment.** The healthiest approach is a **steady, sustainable flow—where you are always refilling and sharing without ever feeling depleted.**

✓ When your cup is balanced, you have **clarity, purpose, and fulfillment**—not just for yourself, but for those around you.

✓ You are able to give **genuinely, not out of obligation or guilt.**

✓ You maintain **meaningful relationships** while still honoring your own needs.

In the end, **true balance isn't just about self-care—it's about connection, generosity, and sustainability.**

4. How to Pour Into Your Own Cup
Reconnect With Yourself

The first step to **pouring into yourself** is identifying what truly **fulfills you** on a deep level. Many people go through life **running on autopilot**, prioritizing work, family, and obligations while neglecting the things that once made them feel **excited, inspired, and alive.**

Ask Yourself:

- *What makes me feel most alive?*
- *What do I miss doing that I haven't made time for?*
- *If I had no responsibilities for a day, what would I choose to do?*

Often, people stop doing things that bring them joy because they're **"too busy"** with responsibilities. But **true replenishment comes from reconnecting with your authentic self.**

Example:

- If you once loved **painting** but haven't picked up a brush in years, making time for art could be exactly what refills your cup.
- If you feel happiest when **traveling, learning, or spending time in nature**, prioritize experiences that reconnect you with that joy.
- If you've always wanted to **write a book, learn an instrument, or take up a new hobby**, don't put it off— make space for it now.

Replenishing yourself means making time for **what fuels your spirit, not just what's necessary for survival.**

Set Boundaries

One of the biggest reasons people feel **drained and depleted** is because they don't **protect their energy.** If you're constantly giving your time, attention, and emotional bandwidth to others without **setting limits,** you'll eventually have nothing left for yourself.

Learn to Say No Without Guilt

Saying no to things that drain you means **saying yes** to your peace and well-being. It's not about shutting people out—it's about **prioritizing yourself when needed.**

   Example:
   - Declining a **social event when you need rest** isn't selfish—it's self-respect.
   - Saying no to **extra work** when you're already overwhelmed isn't being lazy—it's maintaining balance.

Limit Access to Your Energy

Not everyone should have **unlimited access** to your time, emotions, and mental space. Some relationships take more than they give, and if you're not careful, they can **drain your cup completely.**

   Example:
   - A friend who **constantly vents negativity** but never asks about your well-being might be draining your cup.
   - A workplace that **expects you to always be available** with no respect for boundaries can leave you mentally exhausted.

Setting boundaries **isn't about pushing people away—it's about preserving your energy for what truly matters.**

Create Replenishing Rituals

Your cup won't stay full unless you **intentionally** refill it. Making replenishment a **daily habit** ensures that you don't constantly feel like you're running on empty. Small, intentional rituals help you stay **grounded, energized, and fulfilled.**

Simple Daily Habits to Replenish Your Energy:

- **Morning journaling or gratitude exercises** to start your day with clarity.
- **Taking a walk in nature without distractions** to clear your mind.
- **Listening to music, podcasts, or audiobooks that uplift you** instead of consuming negative media.
- **Spending time on creative hobbies like writing, painting, or playing music** to nurture your soul.
- **Practicing meditation, deep breathing, or mindfulness** to center yourself.

Example:

- If your mornings feel chaotic, waking up 10 minutes earlier to **journal, stretch, or meditate** could shift your entire mood.
- If social media is draining your energy, replacing **endless scrolling with reading, listening to a podcast, or learning something new** can leave you feeling inspired instead of exhausted.

- If you always put off hobbies because you're "too busy," scheduling even **30 minutes a week** for something creative can bring back joy and balance.

Even **small acts of replenishment create long-term fulfillment.** The key is **consistency**—filling your cup **regularly, not just when you're already drained.**

Pouring Into Yourself is a Lifestyle

Replenishing your energy isn't a **one-time fix**—it's a lifestyle. The more you pour into yourself **intentionally**, the more you'll have to give **freely and joyfully** to the people and responsibilities in your life.

✓ When you reconnect with what makes you feel alive, you stop feeling stuck.

✓ When you set boundaries, you prevent burnout before it happens.

✓ When you make replenishment a habit, you stay full—without waiting until you're empty.

Your cup should never be **so empty that you're running on fumes,** but it also shouldn't be **so full that you stop sharing your energy with the world.** Balance is the key.

Make time for what fuels you, protect your energy, and watch how everything else in your life falls into alignment.

5. Pouring and Balance in Relationships
How It Affects Others

When your cup is full, your **relationships improve** naturally because you're not giving from a place of exhaustion or obligation— you're giving from **a place of abundance.**

✓ You can give **without resentment** because you're not running on empty.

✓ You become a **better listener and more patient** in conversations.

✓ You show up as **your best self** in friendships, family, and partnerships.

When you're drained, even the people you love can start to feel like **a burden**—not because you don't care about them, but because **you have nothing left to give.** But when you consistently pour into yourself, you bring **patience, kindness, and presence** into your relationships.

Example:

Imagine you've had a long day, you're exhausted, and someone close to you wants to have a deep conversation. If you **haven't taken any time for yourself,** you might respond with frustration, irritation, or zoning out. But if you **allowed yourself to recharge beforehand,** you approach the conversation with **clarity and patience** rather than exhaustion.

✓ **When you prioritize your well-being, you naturally improve the quality of your relationships.**

Communicate Your Needs

Many people struggle to **set boundaries in relationships** because they fear coming across as distant or selfish. But needing time for yourself **isn't a rejection of others—it's a way to show up better for them.**

If the people in your life **don't understand** why you need alone time, the best way to handle it is through **clear and compassionate communication.**

✓ **Instead of just saying,** "I need space," explain **why** it's important:

"I need a little time to recharge so I can be more present for us later."

This simple shift **removes misunderstanding** and helps loved ones see that your alone time **benefits them too.**

Example:

- Instead of disappearing when you feel overwhelmed, let your partner know: *"I love spending time with you, but I need a little time to recharge so I can be fully present when we're together."*

- If friends always expect immediate responses, you can set a boundary by saying: *"I'm taking some time away from my phone today, but I'll check in with you later!"*

✓ **The more you communicate your needs, the easier it becomes to maintain balance in your relationships.**

The Key to Healthy Relationships: Balance

Relationships thrive when **both people's needs are valued.** If you give too much without refilling, you become **drained and resentful.** If you focus only on yourself, you create **emotional distance.** The key is **a steady flow—giving and receiving in a way that feels sustainable.**

✓ **Pour into yourself first, then give to others without depletion.**

✓ **Communicate your needs so your loved ones understand your balance.**

✓ **Recognize that taking time for yourself strengthens your relationships, not weakens them.**

When you take care of yourself, you don't just feel better—you **love better, listen better, and show up better for the people who matter most.**

A full cup doesn't just benefit you—it overflows into everything and everyone around you.

6. Reflection Exercise: Filling Your Cup

This exercise is designed to help you become more intentional about **replenishing your energy** and maintaining balance in your life. Small, consistent actions can make a **huge** difference in how you feel, function, and show up for yourself and others.

a. Write Down Three Activities That Replenish You

Think about what truly refills your cup—things that bring you **joy, relaxation, or inspiration** rather than just temporary distraction. These should be activities that make you feel **energized, peaceful, or fulfilled.**

Examples:

- Reading a book that stimulates your mind.
- Meditating to clear mental clutter.
- Dancing to your favorite music to lift your mood.
- Journaling to reflect and process your thoughts.
- Going on a walk in nature for fresh air and perspective.
- Practicing a creative hobby like painting, writing, or playing music.

Tip: If you're not sure what replenishes you, think about what used to make you happy before life got busy. Reconnecting with old hobbies or interests can be deeply fulfilling.

b. Identify One Boundary You Can Set to Protect Your Energy

Your energy is **valuable**, and without boundaries, it's easy to become overwhelmed or drained by constant demands from work, family, and social obligations. Setting boundaries isn't about cutting people off—it's about creating **a healthy balance** so you can give without depletion.

Examples:

- No checking work emails after **7 p.m.** to separate work from personal life.
- Saying **"no"** to plans when you need rest, without feeling guilty.
- Limiting time spent with people who drain your energy.
- Turning off phone notifications during personal time.
- Designating a **"quiet hour"** each day for yourself—no distractions.

Tip: Boundaries aren't just about **what you say no to**—they're about **what you say yes to instead.** When you protect your energy, you create space for things that truly matter.

c. Commit to One Daily Ritual That's Just for You

Self-care doesn't have to be complicated. A simple daily ritual, even if it's just **10 minutes**, can make a big difference in keeping your cup full. The key is **consistency.**

Examples:

- **10 minutes of journaling** to start or end your day with clarity.
- **Deep breathing exercises** to reset your nervous system.
- **A morning or evening walk** to clear your mind.

- **Sipping tea or coffee in silence** before checking your phone.
- **Listening to a podcast or music that uplifts you.**
- **Practicing gratitude** by writing down three things you're thankful for.

Tip: Choose something **realistic** and **enjoyable**—it doesn't have to be time-consuming to be effective.

Your Cup, Your Responsibility

This reflection exercise is a **reminder that you have control over your energy and well-being.**

✓ **When you choose activities that replenish you, you stop feeling constantly drained.**

✓ **When you set boundaries, you protect your time and peace.**

✓ **When you commit to daily rituals, you build lasting habits of self-care.**

Filling your cup isn't a **one-time task**—it's a daily practice. The more you make it a **priority**, the better you'll feel, and the more you'll have to give to the people and things that matter most.

Small steps, big impact. Prioritize yourself, and watch your life transform.

Closing the Chapter

Pouring into yourself isn't selfish—it's essential.

An **empty cup** serves no one. It leaves you drained, resentful, and unable to show up fully in your life and relationships.

An **overflowing cup** is excessive. When you focus only on yourself without sharing your energy, you risk isolation and disconnection.

A **balanced cup** allows you to give from a place of **abundance, not obligation.** It ensures that you are **nourished, energized, and present** for both yourself and others.

When you **fill yourself first,** you create the energy, clarity, and purpose to thrive—not just for yourself, but for everyone around you.

True balance is not about extremes—it's about **sustainability, fulfillment, and flow.**

Chapter 7: Observing vs. Judging – The Balance of Understanding

1. Everyone and Everything is Different

The Uniqueness of People and Situations

No two people are **exactly alike**, and no two circumstances are truly identical. Even when two individuals go through the **same situation**, their reactions can be **completely different** based on:

- **Personality** – An extroverted person might seek social support, while an introverted person might withdraw and process alone.
- **Background and upbringing** – Cultural influences, past experiences, and personal history shape how people interpret and respond to challenges.
- **Emotional state at the time** – Someone who feels emotionally strong may see an obstacle as a challenge, while someone already struggling may feel overwhelmed.

Example:

Imagine two people lose their jobs on the same day.

- **Person A** sees it as an opportunity to find something better and immediately starts applying for new positions.
- **Person B** feels like a failure, overwhelmed by fear and uncertainty, struggling to move forward.

Both had the **same experience**, yet their **responses were shaped** by their mindset, life experiences, and emotional capacity.

This is why **judging someone's reaction based on how you would respond** is often misleading. People process life **differently**, and what seems simple to one person can be deeply challenging for another.

The Danger of Overgeneralization

When we assume that **everyone should react the same way** in a given situation, we limit our ability to truly **understand and connect with others.**

Examples of Overgeneralization:

- *"If I can move on quickly after a breakup, anyone should be able to."*
- *"If I can work two jobs and hustle every day, anyone struggling financially just isn't trying hard enough."*

The problem? **This way of thinking ignores individual circumstances.** Not everyone has the same emotional resilience, resources, or external support.

People have **different coping mechanisms, personal struggles, and life factors** that influence their decisions. What works for one person **may not be realistic or possible** for another.

A Better Approach: Observe Without Assuming

Instead of projecting your **own perspective** onto others, approach each situation with **fresh eyes and curiosity.**

Ask yourself:

"What don't I know about this person's experience?"

"How might their background shape their reaction?"

When you **observe without assuming**, you see **beyond your own perspective** and gain a deeper understanding of the people around you.

This shift in thinking **fosters empathy, patience, and true connection.** Instead of expecting others to process life the way you do, you allow space for **individual differences**—which is the key to genuine understanding and meaningful relationships.

2. Observing vs. Judging

What is Observation?

Observation is the ability to **take in information without attaching meaning, assumption, or emotion.** It's about seeing things **as they are** rather than interpreting them through a personal lens.

✓ **Example of Observation:**

- *"This person seems upset."*

This statement is **neutral**—it acknowledges an emotion without assuming the reason behind it.

Observation allows us to **gather facts** before making a judgment, helping us respond with **clarity and understanding** rather than knee-jerk reactions.

What is Judging?

Judging happens when we **assign meaning, value, or assumption** to what we observe—often without enough information. While judgment is a natural human tendency, it becomes a problem when it's based on **assumptions rather than facts.**

Example of Judgment:

- *"This person is upset because they're ungrateful."*

This shifts from a neutral **observation** to a **personal interpretation** that may not be true. It assumes **the cause of their emotions** without considering alternative explanations.

Judgment becomes problematic when it leads to **misunderstandings, false conclusions, and unnecessary conflict.**

Balancing the Two

Judgment **isn't inherently bad**—it's how we make decisions, assess situations, and protect ourselves. The key is to **balance judgment with observation**, so we avoid **jumping to conclusions too quickly.**

When Judgment is Useful:

- Deciding **who to trust** and what situations to avoid.
- Recognizing **patterns of behavior** to determine if someone is reliable or toxic.
- **Setting personal boundaries** based on past experiences.

When Judgment is Harmful:

- When it's based on **assumptions rather than facts.**
- When it leads to **misunderstandings and false conclusions.**
- When it prevents **connection, empathy, and deeper understanding.**

Example: Instead of immediately thinking *"That person didn't text back because they don't care about me,"* try observing first:

"They haven't responded yet. Maybe they're busy, or something else is going on."

This **creates space for curiosity** instead of jumping to a negative conclusion.

The Power of Observing First

When we observe first and judge second, we:

✓ Avoid unnecessary misunderstandings.

✓ Give people the benefit of the doubt.

✓ Respond thoughtfully instead of reacting emotionally.

By practicing **neutral observation**, we make space for **patience, clarity, and emotional intelligence**, leading to **better decisions and stronger relationships.**

3. The Cost of Judging Too Quickly

Misunderstandings

When we judge **without enough information**, we risk completely **misinterpreting** someone's motives, emotions, or intentions. A single **assumption** can create unnecessary tension, leading to **misunderstandings that didn't need to happen.**

Example:

You see a coworker who doesn't make eye contact and barely speaks during a meeting.

- **Quick Judgment:** *"They're rude and uninterested."*
- **Observation-First Approach:** *"Maybe they're shy or having a bad day."*

By **not assuming**, you leave space for more possibilities—maybe they're overwhelmed, introverted, or simply preoccupied with personal matters. **Jumping to conclusions too soon limits your ability to truly understand others.**

Missed Opportunities

Quick judgments can also **cause us to write people off too soon**, leading to missed chances for meaningful relationships, friendships, or even career opportunities. We often **judge people based on a single interaction**, assuming we know their character **before truly understanding them**.

Example:

You meet someone at a party who seems standoffish, so you assume they're arrogant and don't bother engaging with them.

Later, you find out they were just **socially anxious in big groups** and actually have a lot in common with you.

Had you taken the time to **observe rather than judge**, you might have formed a great connection. **But by making an instant assumption, you closed the door before the conversation even started.**

Why Slowing Down Matters

By **pausing before forming conclusions**, you:

✓ Give others the benefit of the doubt.

✓ Open the door to deeper understanding.

✓ Avoid unnecessary misunderstandings and misjudgments.

Taking an **observation-first** approach allows you to **see people more clearly, beyond surface-level impressions.** It creates space for **genuine connections, personal growth, and a more open-minded perspective.**

4. How to Stay in Observation Mode
Ask Questions Before Judging

One of the easiest ways to stay in **observation mode** is to **pause and ask questions** before making assumptions. Instead of immediately forming an opinion, take a step back and consider alternative explanations.

Ask yourself:

- *"What might be happening here that I don't see?"*
- *"What else could explain this situation?"*

Example:

Observation: *"They haven't replied to my message today."*

- **Unhelpful Judgment:** *"They must be ignoring me because they don't care."*
- **Helpful Reflection:** *"Maybe they're busy, or something is going on in their life."*

This simple shift **creates space for a more accurate understanding** rather than immediately assuming the worst.

Pause and Reflect

Giving yourself **even a few seconds** before reacting can prevent misjudgments and emotional responses that aren't based on reality.

√ **Tip:** Before jumping to conclusions, take three deep breaths and ask yourself:

- *"Am I seeing this situation clearly?"*
- *"Do I have enough information to make a fair judgment?"*

Taking this pause allows you to **see the bigger picture** before responding impulsively.

Separate Fact from Story

We often take **neutral facts** and unknowingly add **our own interpretations**, turning them into emotional stories that may not be true.

    Example:
- **Fact:** *"They didn't invite me to the event."*
- **Story:** *"They left me out on purpose because they don't like me."*

The fact itself is neutral—it's our **internal narrative** that turns it into something painful or personal. Recognizing when you're **adding a story to a situation** helps you stay in **observation mode** rather than making inaccurate judgments.

The Power of Staying in Observation Mode

✓ Helps you **avoid unnecessary misunderstandings.**

✓ Encourages **better communication and patience.**

✓ Strengthens relationships by allowing for **curiosity instead of assumptions.**

    By making **observation a habit,** you naturally become more **level-headed, understanding, and emotionally intelligent** in your interactions.

5. Judging Yourself
You're Human Too

    We're often our **own worst critics**, holding ourselves to impossible standards and judging ourselves **far more harshly** than we would anyone else. Instead of acknowledging mistakes as part of the learning process, we tend to **internalize them as personal failures.**

    Example of Self-Judgment:

- *"I failed because I'm not good enough."*

A Better Approach:

- *"I made a mistake, but I can learn from it."*

Observing yourself **without self-judgment** leads to **growth instead of self-criticism.** It allows you to see where you can improve **without attacking your self-worth.**

Growth Through Observation

Instead of **labeling yourself** based on a single moment, shift your mindset to **see mistakes as learning experiences.** Every misstep, failure, or setback holds valuable lessons—if you choose to see them that way.

If you notice **negative patterns in yourself**, approach them with **curiosity instead of shame.** Self-judgment keeps you **stuck,** while self-reflection helps you **move forward.**

Ask Yourself:

- *"What can I learn from this situation?"*
- *"How can I respond differently next time?"*

By replacing **judgment with observation**, you create space for **growth, self-compassion, and real progress.**

Why This Matters

- **Judgment keeps you stuck in the past.** Observation helps you move forward.
- **Criticism makes you feel small.** Reflection helps you expand and improve.
- **Self-judgment limits potential.** Self-awareness unlocks it.

By learning to **observe yourself with kindness**, you allow space for the same **understanding and grace** you extend to others. You are **human**—and that means **growing, evolving, and learning** every step of the way.

6. Thriving Through Differences

Celebrating Uniqueness

Differences aren't **obstacles**—they're **opportunities to learn and grow**. Instead of rejecting perspectives that don't align with yours, see them as **chances to expand your understanding of the world.**

Example:

- A friend with a **different worldview** might challenge your thinking in a way that **helps you grow.**
- A coworker with a **different work style** might introduce you to **more efficient ways of doing things.**
- Someone from a **different culture or background** might share **insights you'd never considered before.**

When you embrace differences instead of fearing them, you open yourself up to **new experiences, deeper connections, and a richer perspective on life.**

Embracing Reactions

Not everyone **processes emotions the same way.** Some people are expressive, while others are reserved. Some react immediately, while others need time to process. **Neither is right or wrong—it's just different.**

Understanding that people **express and experience emotions differently** allows you to show **empathy instead of judgment.**

✓ **Tip:** Instead of expecting people to react the way you would, try accepting their emotions as **valid—even if they're different from yours.**

Imagine a World Without Differences

If **everyone thought, acted, and reacted the same way,** life would be **dull and uninspiring.**

No variety. No creativity. No individuality.

Imagine if:

- **Everyone wore the same clothes.**
- **Everyone had the same hairstyle.**
- **Everyone ate the same food.**
- **Everyone lived the same routine, with no unique experiences.**

We would all be **copies of each other,** instead of **unique individuals with our own stories, ideas, and identities.**

Differences are what **make the world vibrant, creative, and exciting.** They allow us to **share, learn, and evolve** in ways we never could if we were all the same.

The Beauty of Individuality

Instead of resisting differences, **embrace them.** They make life more interesting, relationships more dynamic, and experiences more meaningful.

✓ **Variety sparks creativity.**

✓ **Differences inspire innovation.**

✓ Uniqueness gives life its depth and richness.

By celebrating what makes each person **distinct and valuable**, we don't just tolerate differences—we **thrive because of them**.

7. Reflection Exercise: Observing Without Judging

This exercise will help you become more aware of **your judgments**, challenge assumptions, and shift toward an **observation-first mindset**.

a. Think of a Recent Situation Where You Judged Someone Quickly

Take a moment to reflect on a time when you made a **quick judgment** about someone without having all the facts.

- **What assumptions did you make?**
- **Did you base your judgment on past experiences, personal biases, or emotions?**
- **How might you have approached it differently if you had taken time to observe first?**

Example:

- You assumed a friend was ignoring you because they didn't respond to your text right away.
- Later, you found out they were dealing with something personal and just needed space.
- Had you observed first instead of assuming, you might have responded with understanding instead of frustration.

The goal of this reflection isn't to **criticize yourself** but to recognize patterns and learn from them.

b. For the Next Week, Pause Before Judging

For the next seven days, make a conscious effort to **pause** before jumping to conclusions.

✓ **Before forming a judgment, ask yourself:**

- *"Am I basing this on facts or assumptions?"*
- *"What other possibilities could explain this situation?"*
- *"How would I feel if someone judged me this quickly?"*

Challenge:

- Focus on **observing first.**
- Avoid making assumptions based on limited information.
- Try to see situations **from multiple perspectives** before deciding what to think.

By practicing **pausing before judging**, you develop **patience, open-mindedness, and deeper understanding** in your interactions with others.

c. Think of a Movie or TV Show Where You Judged a Character Too Quickly

Sometimes, we judge fictional characters just as quickly as we judge people in real life. Think about a movie or TV show where you **had a strong opinion** about a character at the beginning—maybe you disliked them, thought they were weak, annoying, or even evil.

Now reflect on how you felt about them **after the movie or series was finished**—after you had seen their **backstory, struggles, and growth.**

Example:

- *You disliked a character because they seemed selfish, but later, you learned they had been deeply hurt and were just protecting themselves.*
- *You thought a character was weak or cowardly, but by the end, you saw their resilience and understood why they acted the way they did.*
- *You saw a villain as pure evil at first, but once their past was revealed, you realized they were a product of their experiences.*

Just like with real people, **first impressions don't tell the full story.**

✓ **What changed your opinion?**

✓ **How did their backstory or character development affect the way you saw them?**

✓ **What does this teach you about the way you judge real people?**

By applying this perspective to **real life**, you can start recognizing that **everyone has a backstory you may not know about.** When you give people the space to reveal who they truly are, you may find **more understanding, compassion, and connection than you expected.**

The more you observe, the more you learn. The less you judge, the more you connect.

Closing the Chapter

Life is full of **diverse people, reactions, and perspectives.** No two experiences are identical, and no two people will see the world in exactly the same way. **That's what makes life rich, dynamic, and worth exploring.**

When we **balance observation with thoughtful judgment**, we create space for **growth, understanding, and stronger relationships.** Instead of rushing to conclusions, we learn to see things **as they are, not just as we assume them to be.**

Differences **aren't meant to divide us**—they're how we **learn, evolve, and thrive.** They bring variety, creativity, and depth to our experiences.

When we approach life with **curiosity instead of assumption**, we open the door to **deeper connections, better decision-making, and true self-awareness.**

The more we observe, the more we understand. The more we understand, the more we grow.

Chapter 8: Balancing Ego – The Dance Between Confidence and Humility

1. Understanding Ego

What is the Ego?

The ego is our **sense of self**—it shapes how we see ourselves, how we interact with the world, and how we define our **worth and identity**. It influences our confidence, our boundaries, and our ambitions.

A healthy ego gives us:

✓ **The confidence** to take up space and pursue our goals.

✓ **The self-respect** to set boundaries and stand up for ourselves.

✓ **The drive to achieve, grow, and push forward.**

But ego is a **double-edged sword**—while it helps us, it can also create **blind spots, resistance to change, and defensiveness**. When left unchecked, it can **distort reality, block personal growth, and strain relationships.**

The Dual Nature of Ego

Ego isn't **inherently good or bad**—it exists on a **spectrum** between **healthy confidence** and **destructive self-importance**.

Positive Ego (Healthy)	Negative Ego (Unbalanced)
Confidence and self-respect	Arrogance and superiority

Advocating for your needs	Dismissing others' perspectives
Taking feedback as growth	Taking feedback as an attack
Standing up for yourself	Feeling the need to "win" at all costs

Example:

- A **healthy ego** allows someone to acknowledge their **worth** without needing constant validation.
- A **fragile ego** may cause **defensiveness**, making someone feel personally attacked even when constructive criticism is given.

2. Why Ego is a Balancing Act

Ego is neither **good nor bad**—it's all about **how you manage it.** Too much, and it becomes a barrier to growth. Too little, and it prevents you from standing in your power. The key is **balance.**

Overinflated Ego: When Ego Becomes Too Dominant

When the ego is **too strong**, it can lead to:

- **Defensiveness** – Reacting negatively to feedback instead of learning from it.
- **Arrogance** – Believing you are always right and dismissing other perspectives.
- **Inflexibility** – Struggling to adapt to new ideas or admit mistakes.

Example:

A manager refuses to take input from their team because they believe, *"I know best."* Instead of improving, they **stagnate, alienate others, and miss opportunities for growth.**

When ego **dominates**, it becomes a **wall** instead of a **bridge**— it blocks self-improvement and isolates you from valuable insights.

Weak Ego: When Self-Worth is Too Fragile

A **lack of ego** can be just as damaging—it creates **self-doubt, insecurity, and people-pleasing tendencies.** Instead of arrogance, this extreme leads to **fear of speaking up, chronic self-criticism, and dependence on external validation.**

- **Over-apologizing** – Feeling the need to say *"sorry"* even when you haven't done anything wrong.
- **Seeking external validation** – Constantly needing others to approve of you.
- **Fear of speaking up** – Avoiding conflict or holding back opinions out of fear.

Example:

Someone avoids sharing an idea in a meeting, worried they'll sound *"stupid."* Meanwhile, someone less informed speaks up and **gets praised for their confidence.**

✓ **Confidence is needed to take chances,** speak up, and be seen and heard.

When ego is **too weak**, you **diminish yourself** instead of embracing your worth.

The Sweet Spot: Confidence + Humility

The **ideal ego** is one that is **strong yet flexible**—rooted in **confidence but open to growth.**

✓ **Confidence** – Knowing your worth **without needing to prove it.**

✓ **Humility** – Being open to learning **without diminishing yourself.**

Balancing ego means valuing yourself **while remaining teachable, adaptable, and self-aware.** It allows you to:

- **Stand your ground** without arrogance.
- **Take feedback constructively** instead of personally.
- **Trust yourself** while staying open to new perspectives.

True strength comes from balance—where confidence and humility work together, not against each other.

3. The Role of Ego in Relationships

Ego plays a **major role** in how we connect with others. When balanced, it **strengthens relationships** by allowing us to communicate with confidence and clarity. But when unchecked, it can **create unnecessary conflict, misunderstandings, and emotional distance.**

Ego as a Barrier

An unchecked ego can **block communication** and **create distance** in relationships by making people **prioritize being right over being understood.** When ego takes control, pride replaces vulnerability, and conflicts become **battles to win** rather than issues to resolve.

Example:

A couple argues, and **neither person wants to apologize first** because their ego doesn't want to "lose."

- Instead of **listening and resolving the issue**, both partners hold onto their pride, allowing **resentment to build.**
- The need to be **"right"** becomes more important than the relationship itself.

When ego turns relationships into a **competition**, no one truly wins.

Ego as a Strength

A **balanced ego** allows you to **express your needs, set boundaries, and communicate clearly—without being defensive or dismissive.** It gives you the confidence to **speak up while still valuing the other person's perspective.**

Example:

Instead of saying, *"You never listen to me!"* (which is aggressive and accusatory), a balanced ego says, *"I feel unheard when I share things with you—can we work on that?"*

- This approach **maintains confidence** while allowing space for mutual understanding.
- It shifts the conversation from **blame** to **collaboration.**

A healthy ego helps you communicate without arrogance or insecurity—it allows you to express your feelings while remaining open to the other person's perspective.

How Ego Impacts Communication

Your ego influences **how you handle disagreements, express your emotions, and receive feedback.**

- **Overinflated ego:** *"I don't need to hear your side—I already know I'm right."*
- **Balanced ego:** *"I believe I'm right, but I'm open to hearing your perspective."*
- **Weak ego:** *"I must be wrong if they disagree with me."*

✓ **When ego is balanced, relationships become healthier, deeper, and more understanding.**

Instead of letting ego **fuel conflicts,** use it to **strengthen communication** by approaching conversations with **confidence and openness, rather than pride or insecurity.**

4. How to Balance Ego

Balancing ego is about **finding the middle ground** between **confidence and humility**—knowing your worth **without arrogance** and staying open to growth **without insecurity.**

a. Cultivate Self-Awareness

Ego can sneak in when we're **not paying attention.** The first step to balancing it is **recognizing when it's helping versus when it's hurting.**

✓ **Ask yourself:**

"Am I acting from confidence or defensiveness?"

"Am I listening to understand or just to respond?"

Example:

- If criticism **instantly makes you defensive**, ask yourself if your ego is **protecting you or blocking growth.**
- If you find yourself **interrupting** in conversations, check if you're listening **to understand or just waiting for your turn to talk.**

The more you **check in with yourself**, the easier it becomes to **adjust your mindset in real time.**

b. Practice Humility

Humility **isn't about diminishing yourself**—it's about recognizing that you don't have all the answers, and that's okay. A **humble mindset** allows you to **learn, grow, and evolve.**

Example:

A student with a growth mindset says:

"I don't know everything, but I'm willing to learn."

- Instead of pretending to be an **expert on everything**, humility helps you **stay open to new insights and perspectives.**
- People who think they **already know everything** stay stuck, while those who **embrace learning keep growing.**

c. Build Genuine Confidence

True confidence isn't based on external validation—it comes from **trusting yourself, knowing your value, and believing in your abilities.**

✓ **Ways to build real confidence:**

- **Reflect on past achievements and growth.** Recognizing how far you've come builds self-assurance.

112

- **Set small, realistic goals** and celebrate progress—confidence grows through consistent wins.
- **Learn new skills** to remind yourself of your capabilities and adaptability.

Example:

Instead of feeling **threatened** by someone else's success, confidence allows you to say:

"Their success doesn't take away from mine."

A balanced ego understands that **growth isn't a competition—** there's room for **everyone to thrive.**

d. Embrace Vulnerability

Letting go of ego means allowing yourself to be seen—**flaws and all.** Vulnerability isn't weakness; it's **real strength.**

✓ **Benefits of Vulnerability:**

- **Strengthens authenticity**—you don't have to put on a mask.
- **Builds deeper connections**—people relate to realness, not perfection.
- **Increases self-trust**—owning your truth makes you stronger.

Example:

Instead of pretending to **have it all together**, a confident leader **admits mistakes** and earns **more respect through authenticity.**

The strongest people aren't those **who never fail**—they're the ones **who own their failures, learn from them, and keep moving forward.**

The Power of a Balanced Ego

✓ Self-awareness keeps ego in check.

✓ Humility keeps you open to learning.

✓ Confidence keeps you grounded in your worth.

✓ Vulnerability keeps you connected and authentic.

When ego is balanced, it becomes a **tool for growth instead of a barrier.**

5. Practical Examples of Ego in Action

Balancing ego isn't just a concept—it shows up in **everyday situations.** Here's how shifting from an **ego-driven reaction** to a **balanced response** can make a difference in your interactions.

Scenario 1: Receiving Feedback at Work

Situation: A manager or coworker gives you constructive criticism about your performance.

Ego-Driven Reaction:

"They're just trying to undermine me."

- This reaction **takes feedback personally** instead of seeing it as a chance to improve.
- Ego steps in to **defend pride rather than embracing growth.**

✓ **Balanced Reaction:**

"This feedback is tough to hear, but maybe there's a silver lining in it."

- Instead of rejecting criticism outright, a balanced ego **looks for the valuable takeaway** hidden within it.

- Even if the feedback is harsh, taking it **with a grain of salt** allows you to **separate useful insights from unnecessary negativity.**

A **balanced response** leads to **growth and self-improvement**, while an **ego-driven response** keeps you **stuck and defensive.**

Scenario 2: Conflict in a Relationship

Situation: You and your partner or friend have an argument, and both of you feel hurt.

Ego-Driven Reaction:

"I'm not apologizing first—they should admit they're wrong!"

- This mindset **turns the conflict into a power struggle**, where pride takes priority over resolution.
- Holding onto being "right" prevents healing and keeps the **cycle of resentment going.**

√ Balanced Reaction:

"It doesn't matter who apologizes first—what matters is resolving this together. Let's find the silver lining in this disagreement."

- A balanced ego **prioritizes connection over winning** an argument.
- It **acknowledges emotions** without letting pride get in the way of moving forward.
- Instead of dwelling on what went wrong, **finding the silver lining** can shift the focus to **how this conflict can strengthen the relationship.**

Being right **doesn't always matter—being understood does.** Relationships thrive on **communication, humility, and compromise.**

Why This Matters

Ego can either **block progress or open doors.** The way you handle situations—whether in work, relationships, or personal growth—depends on **whether your ego controls you or you control it.**

✓ **A strong but balanced ego leads to better decisions, deeper connections, and continuous growth.**

✓ **An unchecked ego creates unnecessary conflict, stagnation, and isolation.**

✓ **Taking things with a grain of salt allows you to navigate challenges without overreacting.**

✓ **Looking for the silver lining helps you turn setbacks into learning opportunities.**

The real strength lies in knowing when to step back, listen, and grow—**rather than letting ego take over.**

6. Reflection Exercise: Your Ego in Balance

This exercise will help you **recognize when ego is influencing your actions, both positively and negatively**, and give you practical ways to **bring it into balance.**

a. Think of a Recent Moment When Your Ego Got in the Way

Reflect on a time when **ego influenced your reaction**—maybe you felt defensive, stubborn, or unwilling to see another perspective.

✓ **Ask yourself:**
- *How did my ego affect the situation?*
- *Did it create conflict, resistance, or distance?*

- *What could I have done differently to find a silver lining?*

Example:

- You got frustrated when someone gave you **constructive criticism**, assuming they were attacking you.
- If you had **taken it with a grain of salt**, you might have **seen the value in their perspective** instead of reacting defensively.

b. Think of a Time When You Used Ego to Push Your Way of Thinking on Someone Else

Sometimes, ego **convinces us that we're right**, leading us to push our opinions onto others—even when it's **not our place** to do so.

Ask yourself:

- *Did I step into a situation where I should have stayed out?*
- *Was I forcing my perspective instead of listening?*
- *Did I assume I knew what was best without considering the other person's experience?*

Example:

- You saw a friend struggling with a decision, and instead of listening, you **insisted they take your advice** because you believed it was the "right" way.
- Later, you realized their situation was **more complex than you assumed**, and they needed support, not instruction.
- Just because **your ego tells you you're right doesn't mean you actually are.**

✓ **Lesson:** Sometimes, the best thing you can do is **step back, listen, and let people figure things out for themselves.**

c. Write Down One Area Where You'd Like to Grow

Where do you **struggle most with ego?** Do you:

- Need to be **more confident** and stop second-guessing yourself?
- Need to **listen without defensiveness** and be open to other perspectives?
- Need to **let go of the need to "win"** every argument?
- Need to **respect others' autonomy** instead of pushing your way of thinking?

Example:

"I want to work on recognizing when to step back instead of assuming I know what's best for someone else."

Recognizing **where you want to improve** is the first step toward a **healthier, more balanced ego.**

d. List Three Actions You Can Take This Week to Practice Balancing Your Ego

Now, commit to **small, intentional steps** that will help you balance ego in daily life.

Examples:

- **Accept feedback without taking it personally.** Instead of assuming criticism is negative, ask yourself, *"What's the silver lining in this feedback?"*
- **Admit when you're wrong instead of defending yourself.** A simple *"You're right, I didn't see it that way"* can strengthen relationships instead of fueling unnecessary conflict.

- **Give a compliment without feeling the need to compare yourself.** Instead of thinking, *"They're successful, so I must not be,"* shift to *"Their success doesn't take away from mine."*
- **Pause before giving advice to someone.** Ask yourself, *"Am I helping, or am I just imposing my beliefs?"*

The goal isn't to eliminate ego—it's to manage it in a way that serves you rather than controls you.

Growth happens when you learn to balance confidence with humility, self-worth with openness, and strength with flexibility.

Closing the Chapter

Your **ego isn't the enemy**—it's a tool. Like any tool, it can **build or destroy**, depending on how you use it. When balanced, ego helps you:

✓ **Stand strong in your self-worth** without needing constant validation.

✓ **Stay open to learning and growth** without feeling threatened by feedback.

✓ **Maintain healthy relationships** by balancing confidence with humility.

Balancing ego means **finding the middle ground**—valuing yourself without **dismissing others**, standing firm in your beliefs while **remaining open to change.**

True strength isn't in **never being wrong**—it's in **knowing your worth while still embracing growth, adaptability, and self-awareness.**

A balanced ego doesn't make you smaller or louder—it makes you wiser.

Chapter 9: The Power of Neutrality – Understanding Without Absorption

1. Opening Yourself Up to the World

The Vulnerability of Openness

The more you open yourself up to **understanding people and the world**, the more you expose yourself to both **beauty and harsh realities.**

When you **observe and empathize**, you gain deeper insights into **human nature**—you recognize kindness, resilience, and love. But at the same time, you also become aware of **negativity, suffering, and cruelty.**

Being open to life means you **feel everything more deeply**—both the **good and the bad.** This can be **empowering**, but it can also become **overwhelming** if you absorb too much of the world's energy.

Example:

- You hear a friend talking about their struggles, and instead of simply **understanding and supporting them**, you **internalize their emotions** as if they are your own.
- Soon, you feel **drained and burdened** by problems that aren't even yours.

This is where **neutrality comes in—not to make you indifferent, but to protect your emotional well-being.**

The Emotional Toll of Absorbing Too Much

When you become **too emotionally involved** in everything you observe, it starts to **take a toll on your mental and emotional health.**

Absorbing negativity too deeply can leave you feeling **drained, anxious, or even hopeless. Clinging to positivity too tightly** can create **unrealistic expectations**, leading to disappointment.

Example:

- If you take in **too much of the world's suffering**, you may feel **powerless to make a difference**, leading to **emotional exhaustion**.
- If you believe **only in constant positivity**, any **setback** can feel like a **personal failure**.

✓ **Finding balance means learning how to care without carrying everything.**

Why Balance Matters

Being open to the world is a **gift**—but only when you learn **how to navigate it wisely.**

✓ **Empathy is powerful, but over-absorption is draining.**

✓ **Awareness is enlightening, but obsessing over negativity is paralyzing.**

✓ **Positivity is uplifting, but unrealistic expectations create frustration.**

True openness isn't about **absorbing everything**—it's about knowing **what to take in, what to let go of, and when to step back for your own well-being.**

2. Why Neutrality is Key

What is Neutrality?

Neutrality is the ability to **observe and understand without becoming emotionally attached** to the outcome.

It doesn't mean you **don't care**—it means you **don't let emotions control your responses.** Instead, you maintain **inner stability**, even in unpredictable or emotionally charged situations.

✓ **Neutrality = Clarity + Emotional Strength**

- Instead of reacting impulsively, **neutrality helps you see things as they are**—not better or worse than reality.
- It allows you to engage **thoughtfully** rather than emotionally, preventing **overreactions or unnecessary stress.**

Why Neutrality Matters

When you stay neutral:

✓ **You make better decisions**—because your emotions don't cloud your judgment.

✓ **You engage meaningfully** without being consumed by external chaos.

✓ **You protect your peace**—by avoiding emotional exhaustion.

Example:

A coworker makes a rude comment toward you in a meeting.

Without Neutrality: You immediately take offense, become defensive, and let it ruin your whole day.

With Neutrality: You recognize that **their reaction says more about them than you**, and you don't let it disturb your inner peace.

Neutrality isn't **passivity**—it's **emotional intelligence.** It's the ability to **respond, not react.**

The Flow of Life: Everything Balances Itself

Just like nature, **everything moves in cycles.**

✓ **What goes up must come down.**

✓ **What goes down must eventually come back up.**

When you understand this, you don't get **too attached to highs** or **too discouraged by lows**—because you know that **both are temporary.**

- When things are going **well**, neutrality keeps you **humble and grounded.**

- When things are **difficult**, neutrality reminds you that **this, too, shall pass.**

Instead of **fighting life's natural flow**, neutrality helps you **ride the waves with stability and clarity.**

True power lies in staying centered—no matter what happens around you.

3. How Neutrality Protects Your Peace
Good or Bad, Don't Take It Personally

People's actions are often a **reflection of their inner world—not yours.**

✓ **A person's anger, rudeness, or negativity** usually stems from their own struggles, not something you did.

✓ **A person's kindness, praise, or generosity** often reflects who they are, not just you.

Example:

- Someone who is **consistently negative** is often projecting their **own unhappiness**, not responding to you personally.

- Someone who is **overly critical** may have grown up in an environment where **nothing was ever good enough**, so they repeat that pattern.

When you realize that **people's reactions belong to them, not you**, you stop taking things **so personally**. Neutrality helps you **detach from emotional projections** and see situations **for what they really are.**

The Weight of Absorption

Absorbing too much **external energy** can leave you feeling:

Exhausted from carrying emotions that aren't yours. **Helpless** because you can't fix everything. **Overwhelmed** by constant emotional highs and lows.

✓ **Neutrality lets you engage with life without drowning in it.**

Example:

- Instead of **taking on a friend's pain** as if it's your own, you listen, support, and offer help **without making their struggles your responsibility.**
- This allows you to be **present and compassionate** without being **emotionally drained.**

Protecting Your Energy

✓ **You can care without carrying.**

✓ **You can be empathetic without absorbing.**

✓ **You can support others without sacrificing your inner peace.**

Neutrality isn't detachment—it's emotional balance. It allows you to stay **compassionate and engaged** while **preserving your own well-being.**

True peace comes from knowing what to hold onto and what to let go of.

4. Practical Ways to Stay Neutral

a. Detach from Outcomes

Focus on what you can control—not what you can't.

Example:

- You can **prepare thoroughly** for a presentation, but you **can't control** how everyone will react.
- Instead of stressing about the outcome, focus on **doing your best.**

✓ **Mantra:** *"I control my effort, not the outcome."*

Why it works:

- When you detach from the outcome, you **free yourself from unnecessary stress** and allow yourself to **stay present in the process.**

b. Observe Without Reacting Immediately

The Pause Method – Take a deep breath before responding.

Example:

- Instead of **snapping back** at a rude comment, pause and ask:
  "Is this worth my energy?"
  "Is their comment a reflection of me or them?"

Why it works:

- **Pausing before reacting** prevents unnecessary emotional involvement.
- It helps you **respond with clarity** instead of reacting impulsively.

c. Reframe Your Perspective

See challenges as lessons, not threats.

Example:

- A disagreement with a friend isn't just an argument—it's a **chance to improve communication.**
- A setback at work isn't just failure—it's a **chance to reassess and grow.**

✓ **Mantra:** *"Everything is an opportunity to learn."*

Why it works:

- Shifting your mindset **reduces frustration and disappointment.**
- Seeing challenges as **lessons rather than personal attacks** helps you stay neutral and adaptable.

d. Set Emotional Boundaries

Support without over-identifying.

Example:

- Be there for a **friend struggling with mental health,** but don't **take on their pain as your own.**
- Care about **social issues,** but don't let the **weight of the world** paralyze you.

✓ **Mantra:** *"I can care without carrying."*

Why it works:

- Emotional boundaries allow you to **stay engaged without being emotionally drained.**

- You can **be supportive** without losing yourself in **someone else's struggles.**

Staying neutral doesn't mean being indifferent—it means **choosing what deserves your energy.** When you practice detachment, pause before reacting, shift your perspective, and set emotional boundaries, you protect **your inner peace while staying engaged with the world.**

Balance is the key—care deeply, but don't carry what isn't yours.

5. Neutrality in Practice

Practicing neutrality in **real-life situations** helps you stay grounded, clear-headed, and emotionally balanced. Here's how shifting from an **emotional reaction** to a **neutral response** can transform everyday interactions.

Scenario 1: Dealing with Criticism

Situation: Someone gives you **negative feedback** about your work, appearance, or decisions.

Emotional Response:

"They're attacking me! I need to defend myself."

- Reacting emotionally makes the **criticism feel personal**, triggering defensiveness and stress.
- The focus shifts to **proving yourself right** rather than **learning or improving.**

Neutral Response:

"Is this criticism helpful? If so, I'll use it. If not, I'll let it go."

- Instead of reacting **impulsively**, you pause and assess: *Is there value in this feedback?*
- If the criticism is **constructive**, you use it for growth.
- If it's **negative or unhelpful**, you **let it go without absorbing it.**

Why it works:

- **Focusing on the message, not the emotion,** makes feedback **useful instead of painful.**
- Neutrality allows you to **filter out noise and take only what benefits you.**

Scenario 2: Handling Praise

Situation: You receive **a compliment, award, or recognition** for your work, appearance, or personality.

Emotional Response:

"I need to keep proving myself to get more praise."

- Praise becomes **a source of validation**, making you **reliant on external approval.**
- Instead of enjoying the moment, you feel pressure to **constantly seek more.**

√ **Neutral Response:**

"This praise reflects my effort, but it doesn't define my self-worth."

- You **accept and appreciate** the recognition without attaching your **entire identity to it.**
- You recognize that **praise is temporary**—your value **exists regardless of external validation.**

Why it works:

- **Enjoying recognition without relying on it** creates **inner stability.**
- It allows you to **appreciate success without fearing failure.**

The Power of Neutrality in Everyday Life

✓ With criticism, you learn without getting hurt.

✓ With praise, you enjoy without becoming dependent.

✓ With both, you stay grounded, balanced, and in control of your emotions.

Neutrality isn't about ignoring emotions—it's about not letting them control you.

6. Reflection Exercise: Cultivating Neutrality

This exercise will help you **develop awareness** of your emotional reactions and practice responding with **neutrality instead of attachment.**

a. Think of a Recent Situation That Affected You Emotionally

Reflect on a **recent moment** where you felt **frustrated, defensive, anxious, or overly excited.**

✓ **Ask yourself:**

- *What emotions came up?* (anger, sadness, fear, pride, excitement)
- *What triggered my reaction?*
- *Did I take something personally that wasn't really about me?*
- *How could I have responded more neutrally?*

Example:

- You received **criticism** at work and felt **defensive.**
- Instead of pausing, you reacted emotionally and **argued your point.**
- A **neutral response** could have been: *"Let me consider this feedback objectively before responding."*

Why it works:

- Identifying **your triggers** helps you recognize when **ego and emotion take over.**
- Reflecting on **how you could have responded differently** trains your mind to **stay neutral in the future.**

b. Practice Observing One Interaction Today Without Forming a Judgment

Today, **choose one interaction** to simply **observe.** The goal is to **notice without reacting** and focus on **facts, not assumptions.**

✓ **What to pay attention to:**

- *What was said?* (the exact words, not your interpretation)
- *How was it said?* (tone, body language, energy)
- *What was the context?* (were they stressed, joking, distracted?)

Example:

- A coworker **responds abruptly** to your question.
- Instead of assuming *"They're rude,"* try *"They might be having a stressful day."*
- You remain **neutral, not absorbing their energy or making it about you.**

Why it works:

- The more you practice **pausing before reacting**, the easier neutrality becomes.
- You gain **clarity and control** over your emotions, rather than letting them control you.

The Power of Practicing Neutrality

✓ **You become less reactive and more mindful.**

✓ **You stop taking things personally.**

✓ **You engage with the world from a place of clarity, not assumption.**

Neutrality isn't about shutting down emotions—it's about understanding them without letting them rule you.

Closing the Chapter

Neutrality isn't **indifference**—it's a **superpower** that allows you to:

✓ **Engage with life** without losing yourself.

✓ **Stay clear-headed** instead of reactive.

✓ **Protect your peace** while remaining present.

When you learn to:

- **Observe with curiosity** instead of judgment,
- **Detach from outcomes** and focus on what you can control,
- **Set emotional boundaries** without shutting yourself off,

...you gain the ability to navigate **life's ups and downs** with **grace, resilience, and inner stability.**

Neutrality isn't about caring less—it's about caring wisely.

Chapter 10: Everyone is Human – Choosing Understanding Over Judgment

1. We're All Navigating Something

The Human Experience

No matter how different people seem on the surface, we all share the same fundamental truth—**we are human.** Every person you meet has their own **internal world** filled with **hopes, fears, dreams, regrets, and struggles.**

✓ Some people **wear their emotions openly**, while others **hide them behind a composed exterior.**

✓ Someone's **success** doesn't mean they don't battle **self-doubt.**

✓ Someone's **silence** doesn't mean they don't have **a lot on their mind.**

It's easy to assume we **know** someone based on what we see, but in reality, we are only seeing a **small fraction** of their full story.

The Unseen Battles

Many struggles are **invisible**—they aren't obvious on the surface.

Example:

A **coworker snaps at you** over something small.

- **First reaction:** *"Wow, they're rude."*
- **Reality:** They might be dealing with **family stress, financial problems, or health concerns.**

A **friend cancels plans last minute.**

- **First reaction:** *"They don't value our friendship."*

- **Reality:** They might be feeling **mentally drained** and need time to recharge.

When we **take things personally**, we create **judgment** instead of **understanding**.

✓ **Instead of assuming, pause and ask:**

- *"What else could be going on that I don't see?"*
- *"If I were in their shoes, how would I feel?"*

Approaching situations with curiosity rather than judgment creates space for **empathy and connection**.

Everyone's Life is Different

No two people **live the same life**, no matter how similar they seem.

✓ We may share **similar experiences**, but our **perspectives, struggles, and emotions** will always be unique.

✓ The more we recognize this, the **less we judge** and the **more we connect**.

Behind every face is a story you haven't read—choose understanding over assumption.

2. The Case for Understanding

Why Understanding Matters

Judgment creates division, but understanding builds connection.

✓ **When we judge:**

- We push people away.
- We assume we are "right" and they are "wrong."

- We close the door to connection.

✓**When we understand:**

- We create space for meaningful relationships.
- We give others the same grace we hope to receive.
- We grow in emotional intelligence and compassion.

Example:

A friend confides in you that they made a **life decision** you don't agree with.

- **Judgment says:** *"That was dumb. I would never do that."*
- **Understanding says:** *"I may not agree, but I can see why they made that choice based on their perspective."*

✓ **Understanding doesn't mean agreeing**—it means seeing people's **humanity**, even when their choices are different from yours.

Understanding vs. Agreeing

Some people hesitate to be **understanding** because they think it means they are **endorsing** someone's actions. **But that's not the case.**

✓ **You can disagree with someone's choice while still seeing their perspective.**

✓ **You can understand why someone is struggling without excusing their behavior.**

Example:

- A friend **stays in a toxic relationship** despite your advice to leave.
- You **don't have to agree** with their decision.

- But you can **understand** that emotions, attachment, and personal fears make leaving difficult.

✓ **A powerful question to ask yourself:**

"Would I want someone to judge me based on one decision without understanding the full picture?"

The Power of Choosing Understanding

- Judgment is easy—understanding takes effort.
- Judgment keeps people distant—understanding brings them closer.
- Judgment assumes—understanding seeks to learn.

The more we understand, the more connected, patient, and compassionate we become.

3. Practical Ways to Be More Understanding

a. Lead with Curiosity, Not Assumption

One of the biggest reasons people **misunderstand each other** is because they assume they **already know everything.**

Instead of assuming, ask questions.

Example:

- **A family member is distant** during a conversation.
- **Judgment:** *"They don't care about what I have to say."*
- **Curiosity:** *"I wonder if they had a rough day. Let me check in."*

✓ **Helpful questions to replace assumptions:**

"Can you tell me more about what's going on?"

"What do you need right now?"

Why it works:

- Assumptions **create walls**, but curiosity **builds bridges.**
- Instead of jumping to conclusions, **leading with curiosity fosters connection.**

b. Pause Before Reacting

Many times, we **judge too quickly** before we have all the facts. Taking a moment to **pause and reflect** prevents **emotional overreactions.**

Example:

- Your **partner doesn't respond** to your text for hours.
- **Instant reaction:** *"They must not care about me."*
- **Neutral approach:** *"Let me wait and see what's going on before assuming the worst."*

Ask yourself:

"Am I reacting to their actions, or my interpretation of their actions?"

Why it works:

- **Our emotions often distort reality.**
- Pausing before reacting helps separate **facts from assumptions.**
- Instead of acting on **impulse**, you give yourself time to **see the full picture.**

c. Remember Your Own Humanity

Think about times when **you were misunderstood.**

Example:

- Maybe you **snapped at someone**, but it had **nothing to do with them**—you were just overwhelmed.
- Maybe you **made a mistake**, but instead of receiving understanding, you got **harsh judgment**.

How did that feel?

Now flip it—**how would it feel if someone offered you patience instead of assumption?**

✓ When you remember your own struggles, it's easier to offer others grace.

Treat people how you want them to treat you.

The Power of Practicing Understanding

✓ **Curiosity builds connection.**

✓ **Pausing before reacting prevents unnecessary conflict.**

✓ **Compassion deepens relationships.**

The more understanding you are, the more you create a world where people feel safe to be themselves.

4. The Ripple Effect of Compassion

Understanding Creates Connection

When you choose **understanding over judgment**, you make people feel:

✓ **Seen.**

✓ **Heard.**

✓ **Valued.**

Example:

- A friend who feels **truly heard** is more likely to **open up**, deepening the bond.
- A coworker who is met with **patience instead of frustration** may feel encouraged rather than discouraged.

Why it works:
- Understanding **creates safe spaces** for people to be themselves.
- It strengthens **relationships, trust, and emotional well-being.**

Compassion is Contagious

When you lead with **understanding**, you inspire others to do the same.

✓ Small acts of **patience** create **waves of kindness.**

✓ Compassion spreads in **communities, workplaces, and families.**

Example:
- One person being **kind in a stressful situation** can **shift the entire energy of a room.**
- A simple **"I see where you're coming from"** can **de-escalate tension** and prevent unnecessary conflict.

✓ **Mantra:** *"Understanding someone costs me nothing, but it can mean everything to them."*

One Small Act of Kindness Can Change Someone's Entire Day
- A **moment of patience** can prevent **someone from feeling dismissed.**
- A **kind word** can be **the highlight of someone's day.**

- A **gesture of understanding** can turn **frustration into peace.**

The ripple effect of compassion starts with you. The more understanding you show, the more it spreads.

5. Being Human Includes You

Forgive Yourself

Just as others are **human and imperfect**, so are you.

✓ **You will make mistakes.**

✓ **You will have off days.**

✓ **You will act out of character sometimes.**

And that's **okay.** Growth isn't about being **perfect**—it's about being **aware, learning, and improving.**

Example:

- You **lose your temper** at a loved one.
- **Judgment:** *"I'm a terrible person."*
- **Understanding:** *"I reacted emotionally. I can acknowledge it, apologize, and do better."*

✓ **Offer yourself the same grace you give others.**

Why it works:

- Self-judgment keeps you **stuck in guilt.**
- Self-understanding allows you to **grow and move forward.**

Balance Understanding with Boundaries

Being **understanding** doesn't mean tolerating **harmful behavior.**

✓ **You can forgive someone** but still choose **not to let them be part of your life.**

✓ **You can be kind** without allowing others to **take advantage of you.**

Example:
- A **friend constantly crosses your boundaries.**
- You can **understand** why they do it (*maybe they weren't taught healthy boundaries*).
- But you can still **set firm limits** to protect your **energy and well-being.**

✓ **Understanding = Compassion + Self-Respect.**

Being Kind to Others Starts with Being Kind to Yourself
- Self-forgiveness leads to self-growth.
- Self-respect leads to healthier relationships.
- Balancing understanding and boundaries creates true emotional strength.

Being human means embracing your flaws, learning from them, and giving yourself the same kindness you give others.

6. Reflection Exercise: Choosing Understanding

This exercise will help you become more aware of judgment, practice curiosity over assumption, and develop compassion for both others and yourself.

a. Think of Someone You've Recently Judged

Reflect on a time when you made an assumption about someone based on their actions, words, or attitude.

✔ **Ask yourself:**

- What might they be navigating that I don't know about?
- Was I assuming their intentions without understanding their situation?
- How can I shift from judgment to curiosity?

Example:

- You thought a coworker was lazy because they kept missing deadlines.
- Later, you found out they were dealing with a personal crisis at home.
- Instead of assuming, you could have checked in or given them space to share.

Why it works:

- This exercise trains your mind to replace assumption with curiosity.
- It helps you develop empathy without jumping to conclusions.

b. Reflect on a Time When Someone Showed You Understanding

Think of a moment when someone gave you grace instead of judgment.

✔ **Ask yourself:**

- How did it feel to be understood instead of criticized?
- Did it change how you saw yourself or the situation?
- How can you extend that same grace to others?

Example:

- You made a mistake at work, but instead of shaming you, your manager said, *"I know you're capable. Let's figure out how to fix this together."*
- That response relieved your stress and made you feel supported instead of attacked.
- Now, you can pay that kindness forward by responding the same way to others.

Why it works:

- Experiencing understanding firsthand makes it easier to offer it to others.
- It reminds you that kindness has power—even in difficult moments.

c. Reflect on a Time Where You Could Have Been More Understanding With Yourself

Think of a moment when you were too hard on yourself—a time when you judged your actions, emotions, or mistakes instead of offering yourself compassion.

✓ **Ask yourself:**

- Did I judge myself for struggling instead of recognizing that I'm human?
- If a friend was in the same situation, would I have treated them the way I treated myself?
- How can I practice more self-understanding in the future?

Example:

- You didn't meet a personal goal, and instead of recognizing your effort, you told yourself, *"I failed. I'm not good enough."*

- Looking back, you realize you were doing your best with the energy and knowledge you had at the time.
- Next time, instead of being self-critical, you can say, *"I'm learning. I'll do better next time."*

Why it works:
- Practicing self-understanding builds self-worth.
- The way you speak to yourself shapes your confidence and resilience.

Understanding is a Choice

✓ You choose to replace judgment with curiosity.

✓ You choose to offer others the same grace you've received.

✓ You choose to be kind to yourself, even when you don't feel like you deserve it.

Understanding isn't just about how you treat others—it's about how you treat yourself, too.

Closing the Chapter

At the end of the day, **we're all just human.**

We all have **stories, struggles, victories, and regrets**—and no one is perfect.

Choosing **understanding over judgment** creates:

✓ **Peace** within yourself and in your relationships.

✓ **Connection** that bridges differences and brings people closer.

✓ **Personal growth** that allows you to see beyond assumptions and into the truth of human experience.

Seeing the **humanity in others** makes the world **less divided** and more **compassionate.**

✓**Understanding is a gift you can give freely**—and it always starts with **seeing the humanity in yourself and others.**

When we understand each other, we build a world where kindness, patience, and connection can thrive.

Chapter 11: Owning Your Humanity – Growth Through Self-Awareness and Acceptance

1. The Weight of Mistakes

When You Behave in a Way You Shouldn't

Everyone has moments where they **act out of character**—whether it's:

✓ Snapping at a loved one.

✓ Making a selfish decision.

✓ Avoiding responsibility.

✓ Letting emotions dictate actions instead of reasoning.

These moments can feel **heavy**—sometimes leading to **shame, regret, or self-judgment.**

But here's the truth:

✓ **One bad moment doesn't define you.**

✓ **Mistakes are opportunities for growth.**

Example:

- You **lose your temper** during an argument and say something you regret.

- **Judgment-based thinking:** *"I'm a terrible person."*

- **Growth-based thinking:** *"I lost control in the moment—how can I handle it better next time?"*

✓ **Reframing mistakes as learning moments** stops them from becoming **self-sabotage.**

Shame vs. Growth

Shame keeps you stuck. Growth moves you forward.

- **Shame-based thinking:** *"I messed up, so I must be bad."*
- **Growth-based thinking:** *"I made a mistake, but I can learn from it."*

Example:

- You let your **insecurity** get in the way of celebrating a friend's success.
- **Shame:** *"I'm such a jealous person."*
- **Growth:** *"I was struggling with my own self-worth. Next time, I'll focus on celebrating them without comparing."*

✓ **Self-awareness should be a tool for improvement—not self-punishment.**

A Better Question to Ask Yourself:

"How can I grow from this, instead of beating myself up?"

- Mistakes don't mean **you are bad**—they mean you are **human.**
- Growth happens when you **acknowledge, reflect, and improve.**
- **The goal isn't to be perfect—it's to be better than yesterday.**

Your past mistakes don't define you. How you learn from them does.

2. Balancing Accountability with Self-Compassion
You're Human Too

Just as you **extend grace and understanding to others**, you deserve that same grace.

✓ **You are allowed to mess up and still be a good person.**
✓ **Growth isn't about perfection—it's about progress.**

Example:

- If a **friend** came to you feeling guilty about how they reacted in a situation, you wouldn't say, *"You're awful."*

- So **why do we say that to ourselves?**

✓ **Self-compassion allows you to take accountability without self-destruction.**

Owning vs. Overthinking

There's a **difference between self-awareness and self-punishment.**

- **Healthy accountability** = Acknowledging mistakes and learning from them.

- **Overthinking** = Holding onto guilt long after the lesson has been learned.

Example:

- You **regret something you said** in a heated moment.

- **Healthy approach:** *"I'll apologize and reflect on how I can do better next time."*

- **Overthinking:** *"I replay it over and over in my mind, feeling like a terrible person."*

✓ **A mistake is a moment, not a life sentence.** The lesson is meant to guide you, not haunt you.

A Better Question to Ask Yourself:

"What's one action I can take to improve, and how can I let the rest go?"

✓ Accountability means learning from the past.

✓ Self-compassion means not living in it.

You don't erase mistakes by punishing yourself—you erase them by growing from them.

3. Defining Your Fulfillment

What Brings You Joy?

Fulfillment is deeply personal—it doesn't look the same for everyone. What brings one person **happiness and purpose** might not resonate with another—and **that's okay.**

✓ Your path doesn't have to look like anyone else's.

✓ Happiness isn't one-size-fits-all.

Example:

- One person might find **fulfillment** in **building a family.**
- Another might feel fulfilled through **art, travel, or career growth.**
- Someone else might find it in **helping others or mastering a skill.**

Neither is more **"correct"**—**fulfillment is about what speaks to your soul.**

Reflection Questions:

✓ What makes you feel alive?

✓ What would you still do, even if no one else noticed or cared?

✓ How can you prioritize those things more in your life?

Why this matters:

- The world will always tell you what **should** make you happy.

- **Real fulfillment comes from knowing yourself—not following someone else's definition of success.**

Your happiness is yours to define, create, and protect.

4. Everyone's Needs Are Unique

Understanding Your Needs

Personal needs aren't universal—what works for you **may not work for someone else.**

✓ Some people **recharge in solitude**—others thrive in **social interaction.**

✓ Some people need **structure and routine**—others crave **spontaneity and freedom.**

Example:

- You might find peace **being alone with a book,** while a friend finds their energy **in large social gatherings.**

- One isn't "better" than the other—it's just **different.**

✓ **When you understand your own needs, you stop forcing yourself into a mold that doesn't fit.**

Don't Impose Your Fulfillment on Others

Just because **something brings YOU happiness,** doesn't mean it will bring happiness to others.

Example:

- You **LOVE working out** and feel amazing after a gym session.
- But that doesn't mean **everyone else** will enjoy it the same way.
- A friend finds fulfillment in **meditation and quiet mornings**, but that might **not work for you.**

✓ Sharing is beautiful, but respecting differences is essential.
Better mindset:
"I love this, but it's okay if others don't."

The Perks of Liking Something Others Don't

Other people not liking the things you like can actually be a good thing!

Example:

- If you're the **only one in your home** who likes a particular snack, **whenever you go to get one, it'll always be there!**
- If you love **a niche hobby or interest**, you might get **a sense of personal uniqueness and identity from it.**

✓ **Your preferences make you unique, and that's something to embrace.**

Embracing Individuality

✓ **Understanding yourself** means embracing what truly makes you happy.

✓ **Understanding others** means respecting their path, even if it's different from yours.

✓ The world thrives on diversity—what fulfills one person might be completely different from another, and that's what makes life interesting.

True fulfillment is found in embracing what works for you while allowing others the freedom to do the same.

5. Thriving Through Differences

Why Differences Matter

If everyone was the same, **life would be dull.**

✓ **Differences create balance, contrast, and growth.**

✓The people around you can **challenge, inspire, and complement** you in ways you wouldn't expect.

Example:

- A friend who is **super logical** might help you see things **from a different perspective.**
- A partner who is **more relaxed** might **balance out your high-energy personality.**

✓ **Instead of seeing differences as obstacles, embrace them as opportunities for learning.**

Celebrate, Don't Compare

Your path isn't meant to look like anyone else's.

✓ **Comparison leads to frustration—but appreciation leads to growth.**

Example:

- Instead of thinking, *"They're so far ahead of me in life,"* shift to:

  "Their journey is different from mine, and that's okay."

Better mindset:

"My path is mine to walk, and it doesn't have to match anyone else's."

The Beauty of Individuality

✓ Differences make life more interesting.

✓ Your strengths might be someone else's weaknesses—and vice versa.

✓ Instead of competing, we can complement and learn from each other.

Embracing differences doesn't just help you grow—it helps you thrive.

6. Reflection Exercise: Owning Your Humanity

This exercise will help you **acknowledge your growth, define your fulfillment, and embrace differences with an open mind.**

a. Think of a Moment When You Behaved in a Way You're Not Proud Of

Ask yourself:

- *What triggered that behavior?* (Stress? Fear? Insecurity?)
- *What can you learn from it?*

Example:

- You **snapped at a friend** because you were overwhelmed.
- Instead of just feeling guilty, reflect: *"Next time, I can communicate that I need space instead of reacting impulsively."*

✓ Growth happens when you reflect, not when you dwell.

b. Write Down Three Things That Bring You Fulfillment

✓ **What activities, experiences, or moments make you feel truly alive?**

Example:

- **Creativity** (painting, writing, music)
- **Nature & Movement** (walks, workouts, fresh air)
- **Connection** (deep conversations, quality time with loved ones)

How can you incorporate them into your daily or weekly routine?

- Can you set aside **15 minutes a day** or **one day a week** for these things?
- Can you **replace time spent on unfulfilling activities** with things that bring you joy?

Prioritizing fulfillment isn't selfish—it's necessary.

c. Reflect on a Time When Someone Else's Differences Challenged You

✓ **Ask yourself:**

- *What did you learn from that experience?*
- *Did their perspective help you grow, even if you didn't agree?*
- *How can you embrace differences more openly in the future?*

Example:

- A coworker's **way of thinking clashed with yours**, and it frustrated you.
- But stepping back, you realized **their perspective had value**—they challenged you to **think in a way you wouldn't have on your own.**

✓ **Better mindset:**

"I don't have to agree with everyone, but I can learn from anyone."

Closing the Chapter

Growth starts with **awareness.**

✓ **Acknowledging your flaws** helps you improve.

✓ **Recognizing your fulfillment** helps you prioritize joy.

✓ **Embracing differences** helps you grow in wisdom and understanding.

Owning your humanity means **accepting that you're imperfect**—just like everyone else.

✓ **You will make mistakes.**

✓ **You will have regrets.**

✓ **You will have to work on yourself.**

And **all of that is okay.**

Growth happens when you balance **self-awareness with self-compassion.** Thriving isn't about **being like everyone else**—it's about embracing **your unique path** while respecting the paths of others.

You don't have to be perfect. You just have to be real.

Chapter 12: The Journey Within – Listening to Yourself

1. Why Active Listening Starts with You

Your Inner World Reflects Your Outer World

The way you **experience life** starts with how you **treat yourself.**

If your **inner world is chaotic**, it's hard to find **peace** in the world around you.

If your **mind is constantly cluttered**, everything in your life will feel **overwhelming.**

If you **ignore your own needs**, you'll struggle to make **decisions that truly serve you.**

Example:

- Imagine trying to listen to **music** while five different songs play at the same time.
- This is what it's like when you **ignore your own voice** and let the noise of others **dictate your life.**

When you take the time to listen to yourself, you gain:

- **Clarity**—You understand what you truly want.
- **Direction**—You stop second-guessing your decisions.
- **Peace**—You detach from external chaos.

The Foundation of Fulfillment

If you don't take the time to **understand your own needs, emotions, and desires**, how can you expect to live a **fulfilling life?**

Too often, people seek answers **outside of themselves**, looking for validation, guidance, or direction from others.

The real answers—the ones that truly matter—are already **within you.**

Example:

Ignoring your gut feelings might lead you to:

- A **career** that drains you.
- A **relationship** that doesn't align with your values.
- A **life** that feels like it belongs to someone else.

✓ **Better question to ask yourself:**

"Am I making this choice because it's right for me, or because I think I should?"

When you start listening to yourself first, life starts making sense.

Your intuition is your greatest guide—when you learn to trust it, everything falls into place.

2. The Answer is Already Inside You

Trusting Your Gut Feeling

Your **intuition is your inner compass**—it knows what's best for you, often before your **logical mind** catches up.

It's that **feeling of hesitation** before saying yes to something that doesn't align with you.

It's the **sudden clarity** you get about a decision, even when you can't explain why.

Example:

- Have you ever **met someone** and immediately felt something was **off?**
- Or walked into a place and felt an **instant sense of peace or discomfort?**

156

That's your **gut speaking.** It picks up on **subtle signals** that your mind might miss.

When you ignore your intuition, you often regret it later.

When you trust it, you avoid unnecessary stress and misalignment.

Silencing the Noise

The world is filled with **opinions, expectations, and advice—** but the loudest voice should always be **your own.**

Social media, family, friends, and society all have opinions on what you should do.

At the end of the day, **you're the only one who has to live with your choices.**

Example:

- Someone tells you to take a **"safe" job** instead of following your passion.
- If you listen to them over yourself, you may find yourself feeling **stuck and unfulfilled.**

√ **Better mindset:**

"I can listen to advice, but my final decision must come from what feels right to me."

Your True Path is Already Within You

Your intuition is always guiding you—you just have to listen. When you block out the noise and trust yourself, life starts to feel aligned.

The answers you seek aren't "out there"—they've been within you all along.

Your gut feeling is your truth—trust it, and it will never lead you astray.

3. Health is Wealth

Taking Care of Your Vessel

Your body and mind are your greatest tools—when they're in balance, everything flows more easily.

Sleep, nutrition, and movement aren't just self-care—they're acts of self-respect.

When you neglect your body, your mind suffers too.

Example:

- Lack of sleep makes it harder to think clearly.
- Eating poorly leaves you feeling sluggish and unfocused.
- Not moving your body traps stress and emotions inside.

✔ **Better question to ask yourself:**

"Am I treating my body in a way that supports my best self?"

When you nurture your body, you nurture your mind.

The Mind-Body Connection

Your thoughts, emotions, and body are deeply connected. A calm, well-rested body helps you hear your inner voice more clearly.

Example:

- **Ever notice how stress shows up physically?**
- **Tight shoulders**
- **Headaches**
- **Fatigue**
- **It's all connected. Your body absorbs what your mind feels.**

✔ **Better habit:**

"Check in with your body regularly—what is it telling me?"

Your Well-Being is Your Foundation

A strong mind needs a strong body.

Your energy, clarity, and emotions are all tied to how you treat yourself.

When you take care of yourself physically, mentally, and emotionally, you create space for clarity and peace.

Your health is your greatest wealth—invest in it daily.

4. This is Your World

Your Reality is Unique

Everyone is living in their own version of the world, shaped by their:

✓ **Experiences.**

✓ **Beliefs.**

✓ **Perspectives.**

Example:

- Two people can experience the **same event** and interpret it **completely differently.**
- One might see an **opportunity.**
- The other might see a **setback.**

Better mindset:

"I don't have to see the world the way others do—I can create my own reality."

The Only Person Who Truly Knows You is You

No one else fully understands your **thoughts, emotions, or dreams.** You are the **only one** who knows what truly fulfills you.

    Example:

- If **something feels right** to you, it **doesn't matter if others don't understand.**
- If **something feels wrong** to you, **trust that feeling—even if no one else sees it.**

    ✓ **Mantra:**

"I am the expert of my own life."

You Create Your Own Reality

    You are not here to live someone else's story—you are here to create your own.

    Your perspective is yours to shape, and your path is yours to walk.

The more you trust yourself, the more aligned your life will feel.

    This is your world—make it one that feels right for you.

5. Embracing Solitude

Don't Be Afraid to Be Alone

Solitude is where self-discovery happens.

When you're alone, you can **hear yourself clearly** without outside influences.

    Example:

- Spending time **journaling or meditating** can reveal insights you didn't know you had.

    ✓ **Better habit:**

"Create time for silence daily, even if it's just 10 minutes."

Learning to Love Your Own Company

✓ If you don't enjoy your own company, **how can you expect others to?**

✓ Nurture yourself **as you would a close friend**—with **patience, kindness, and attention.**

   Example:

 • Take yourself **on a solo date**—learn to enjoy your own presence.

   ✓ **Better mindset:**
"I am enough for myself."

The Relationship Between Solitude and Stability

   ✓ How can you expect other people to like being around you if you don't like yourself?

   ✓ And vice versa—if you deeply enjoy your own company, you naturally attract others who value you.

   A person who cannot sit alone is often deeply unstable—constantly running away from their problems and, ultimately, their solutions.

   ✓ Solitude forces you to face yourself—and that's where true growth happens.

   Being alone isn't loneliness—it's self-mastery. When you learn to love solitude, you unlock true confidence, peace, and independence.

6. Practical Tools for Listening to Yourself
Gut Check Practice

Ask yourself:

"What feels right in my gut?"

"Am I doing this because I want to or because I think I should?"

✓ **Why it works:**

- Helps you **differentiate between external pressure and internal truth.**
- Strengthens your ability to **trust your instincts.**

Daily Quiet Time

Spend 10 minutes journaling, meditating, or just sitting with your thoughts.

Why it matters:

- When you remove **outside noise**, your inner voice becomes clearer.
- Helps you process emotions and **gain clarity on what you truly feel.**

Body Awareness Scan

Notice areas of tension or discomfort—your body often holds emotional messages.

Example:

- **Tight shoulders?** You might be carrying stress.
- **A heavy chest?** Unprocessed emotions could be weighing you down.
- **A gut feeling?** Your intuition might be trying to tell you something.

✓ **Why it matters:**

- Your body often signals **what your mind ignores.**

- Learning to **read your body's signals** helps you understand yourself on a deeper level.

Listening to Yourself is a Skill

✓ The more you **check in with yourself**, the clearer your inner voice becomes.

✓ Small daily habits—**gut checks, quiet time, body awareness**—strengthen your ability to **trust your own guidance.**

✓ **The answers you seek aren't outside of you—they're already within.**

Your body, mind, and intuition are always speaking to you—make sure you're listening.

7. Reflection Exercise: Your Inner World

a. Write Down 3 Moments When You Trusted Your Gut and It Worked Out

✓ **Think back to times when you listened to your intuition and it led you in the right direction.**

Questions to reflect on:

- What happened in those moments?
- How did it feel to trust yourself?
- What did those experiences teach you about your intuition?

Why this matters:

- Recognizing these moments **reinforces your trust in yourself.**
- Helps you see that your gut feeling is often **more reliable than overthinking.**

b. Reflect on What Makes You Feel Most at Peace

✓ **Think about the times when you feel completely at ease.**

Questions to reflect on:

- What activities, places, or people bring you the most peace?
- How often do you allow yourself to experience those moments?
- How can you prioritize them more in your daily or weekly life?

Why this matters:

- When you know what brings you peace, you can **intentionally create more of it in your life.**
- Helps you identify **what truly fulfills you versus what drains you.**

c. List One Way You Can Nurture Yourself This Week

✓ **Self-care isn't just about bubble baths—it's about giving yourself what you need.**

Ideas:

- Take a break when you feel overwhelmed.
- Do something creative—paint, write, dance, or play music.
- Simply rest—give yourself permission to recharge without guilt.

Why this matters:

- Small acts of self-care **strengthen your relationship with yourself.**
- **Listening to your needs and responding to them is the foundation of self-trust.**

Closing the Chapter

Your **inner world** is your **sanctuary, your guide, and your strength.** The more you **trust yourself,** the more aligned your life feels. When you **prioritize peace and self-nurturing,** you gain **clarity, confidence, and fulfillment.**

✓ **Trust yourself.**

✓ **Nurture your well-being.**

✓ **Live in alignment with who you truly are.**

The answers you seek **aren't outside of you—they've been within you all along.**

The journey within is the most important one you'll ever take. When you truly listen to yourself, you start creating a life that feels right for you.

Chapter 13: Your "Why" – The Anchor in Hard Times

1. The Importance of a "Why"

Your Guiding Light

Life is unpredictable—there will be moments when things feel overwhelming, when you question everything, and when you wonder if you have the strength to keep going.

✓ In those moments, your **"why"** becomes your **guiding light**—the thing that keeps you grounded, no matter how chaotic life gets.

✓ It reminds you that your **life has purpose**, even when circumstances feel unfair or unbearable.

Example:

- Someone might find their **"why"** in their **faith in God**, believing that every hardship has meaning and that they are being guided.
- Another person's **"why"** might be **their family**, knowing that their children depend on them.

✓ **When life tests you, your "why" is what keeps you moving forward.**

Fuel for Resilience

A **"why"** doesn't magically erase hardship, but it gives you the **strength to endure it.**

✓ It helps you push through pain, disappointment, and obstacles because **you're fighting for something bigger than the struggle itself.**

Example:

- A student working two jobs while studying late at night reminds themselves that their **"why"** is to create a better future.
- An athlete training through injuries pushes forward because their **"why"** is to prove to themselves that they are stronger than their circumstances.

✓ **When your "why" is strong enough, no challenge can break you.**

2. Finding Your "Why"

What is a "Why"?

Your **"why"** is the driving force behind everything you do. It is:

✓ **Your purpose.**

✓ **Your anchor.**

✓ **Your reason for pushing forward.**

It's deeply personal—**no two people have the same "why."** It can be **spiritual, emotional, practical, or deeply personal.**

Examples of Different "Whys":

- **Faith as a "why":** Someone may believe that **God has a plan for them**, giving them strength in difficult times.
- **Passion as a "why":** Another person's purpose might be **helping others**, creating something meaningful, or leaving a legacy for their family.
- **Self-growth as a "why":** Some people are driven by a **desire to evolve, learn, and experience life fully.**

✓ **No "why" is too small or too big—what matters is that it speaks to you.**

Reflection Questions to Find Your "Why"
Ask yourself:
What gives my life meaning?
When things get hard, what keeps me going?
Who or what inspires me to show up as my best self?
If I lost everything tomorrow, what would still matter to me?

Your "Why" is Already Within You
✓ You don't have to **search for it outside of yourself.**
✓ It's been **guiding you all along—you just need to uncover it.**
✓ When you **connect with your "why,"** you gain clarity, motivation, and a deep sense of fulfillment.

   Your "why" is the foundation of your purpose—when you find it, everything else falls into place.

3. The Balance of Having Yourself + Your "Why"
Why Both Are Essential
✓ **You are your foundation, but your "why" is your fuel.**
✓ **Without self-awareness, you might feel lost.**
✓ **Without a "why," you might feel unmotivated.**
   Example:
   - **Knowing yourself** gives you clarity about what you truly want.
   - **Your "why"** gives you the motivation to **pursue it.**
      ✓ **Together, they create balance.**

Your "Why" as Your Focus

When life feels overwhelming, your **"why" provides direction.**

√ **It's the lighthouse guiding you through the storm.**

√ **It reminds you that every struggle is temporary, but your purpose is not.**

Example:

- Someone **battling depression** might remind themselves that their "why" is simply to **make it to tomorrow—to see another sunrise.**
- For some, the **"why" might be their family, their faith, or the chance to create something meaningful.**

√ **Sometimes, survival is enough.** Your "why" doesn't have to be **grand—it just has to be real.**

When You Have Yourself + Your "Why"

- **You stay grounded in who you are.**
- **You stay focused on what matters most.**
- **You build a life that feels meaningful and fulfilling.**

When you know yourself and have a "why," you can face anything life throws at you.

4. Examples of a "Why" in Action

a. Faith

√ Many people, like you, find strength in **God** or a **spiritual belief.**

√ Faith offers **hope, perspective, and a sense of connection to something greater.**

Example:

- A person going through **a difficult season** might find comfort in **prayer, scripture, or surrendering their struggles to God.**
- Even in **uncertainty, faith provides reassurance** that there is a **greater plan at work.**

b. Family

✓ A parent might find their "why" in **providing a stable and loving life for their children.**

Example:

- A **single mother working multiple jobs** reminds herself, *"I'm doing this so my kids never have to struggle the way I did."*
- A person caring for a sibling or parent finds motivation in **showing up for those they love.**

✓ **Family can be a powerful motivator to keep going.**

c. Personal Growth

✓ Some people are driven by a **desire to evolve, heal, or prove something to themselves.**

Example:

- A person who **overcame childhood trauma** might dedicate their life to **breaking generational cycles.**
- Someone training for a **marathon** isn't just running for fitness—they're **proving to themselves that they are capable of more than they ever imagined.**

✓ Sometimes, your "why" is simply to be the best version of yourself.

Your "Why" is Your Power

- No matter what your "why" is, it keeps you anchored when life gets hard.
- It reminds you of what truly matters.
- It gives you the strength to keep going, even when you don't feel like it.

Your "why" is the reason you rise every morning—embrace it, nurture it, and let it guide you forward.

5. Strength in Hard Times

Your "Why" Doesn't Have to Be Grand

✓ Your "why" **doesn't need to be life-changing**—it just needs to **keep you going.**

✓ It can be something **as simple as wanting to see another sunrise** or finding joy in **small daily moments.**

Example:

Someone battling **depression** might remind themselves:
"My dog needs me."

"I want to see how my favorite show ends."

✓ **No "why" is too small—if it keeps you going, it matters.**

Your "Why" Evolves

As you **grow, change, and experience life,** your "why" may **shift—and that's okay.**

What mattered to you at **18 might change by 30,** and that's a sign of growth.

Example:

- A person's **"why" might start as proving something to others** but later evolve into **doing things for themselves.**
- A career-driven person may later find that **their true "why" is balance, family, or inner peace.**

✓ The only rule is that your "why" must stay authentic to you.

Your "Why" is Always There

✓ Even when life feels heavy, your "why" **can be the small spark that keeps you moving forward.**

✓ Whether it's **big or small, temporary or lifelong,** your "why" is yours—and that makes it powerful.

No matter how hard life gets, if you have a "why," you will always have a reason to keep going.

6. Practical Steps to Strengthen Your "Why"

a. Daily Reminders
Write down your "why" and keep it visible.

Place it on your **phone, desk, or mirror** so you see it every day.

Example:
- If your **"why" is family,** keep a **photo of them** where you can see it daily.
- If your **"why" is personal growth,** write a quote or affirmation that inspires you.
  Why it works:
- Keeps your **purpose in front of you**, even on tough days.
- Reinforces your **motivation and focus** throughout the day.

b. Reconnect Regularly

Set aside time weekly to reflect on your "why."

Ask yourself: *"Is my daily life aligned with my purpose?"*

Example:

- If your **"why" is health**, but your **habits don't reflect that,** it's time to **refocus.**
- If your **"why" is making an impact,** check in—**are your actions moving you closer to that goal?**

Why it works:

- Helps you **stay aligned** instead of getting caught up in distractions.
- Keeps your **"why" strong and adaptable** as you grow.

c. Share Your "Why" with Others

Saying your "why" out loud makes it more real.

Surround yourself with **people who support your "why."**

Example:

- If your **"why" is starting a business**, tell a **trusted friend** so they can **hold you accountable.**
- If your **"why" is self-improvement,** discuss it with someone who **inspires you.**

✓ **Why it works:**

- Speaking it into existence **reinforces your commitment.**
- Supportive people **remind you of your "why"** when you lose sight of it.

Strengthening Your "Why" Strengthens You

✓ Daily reminders keep you focused.

✓ Reflection ensures alignment.

✓ Speaking your "why" gives it power.

Your "why" is the fuel behind your purpose—nurture it, and it will carry you forward.

7. Reflection Exercise: Discovering Your "Why"

This exercise will help you **gain clarity** on what truly drives you, especially in difficult times.

a. Write Down What Motivates You During Tough Times

✓ When things get hard, **what keeps you from giving up?**

✓ Is it **faith, family, personal growth, or something else?**

Example:

- "I keep going because I believe God has a purpose for me."
- "I push through challenges because I want to build a better future for my family."
- "I remind myself that I've overcome obstacles before, and I can do it again."

Why this matters:

- Helps you **identify patterns** in what keeps you strong.
- Strengthens your **awareness of what truly matters to you.**

b. Think of a Moment When Life Felt Hard, But You Kept Going

✓ **What was your "why" in that moment?**

Example:

- When struggling through **a difficult job, heartbreak, or personal loss,** what kept you moving forward?

- Maybe it was the **desire to see a better future** or the **people who count on you.**

Why this matters:

- Recognizing your **resilience** reminds you that your "why" has been guiding you all along.

c. If Your "Why" Feels Unclear, Ask Yourself:

What or who would I fight for, no matter what? What brings me joy, even in small doses?

   Example:

- If you had **nothing left**, what would still matter?
- Is it **a loved one, a dream, a belief, or even just the desire to experience more of life?**

Why this matters:

- Your "why" doesn't have to be **huge or obvious**—sometimes, it's as simple as wanting to see what happens next.

Your "Why" is Already Within You

✓ **It has carried you through your hardest days.**

✓ **It will continue to guide you, even when the path isn't clear.**

✓ **When you find it, nurture it, and trust it—it will always lead you forward.**

No matter where you are in life, your "why" is your foundation. Keep it close, and it will never let you fall.

Closing the Chapter

Your **"why"** is your **anchor, your fuel, and your light** in the darkest moments.

✓ Whether it's **faith, family, or personal growth**, it keeps you moving forward when the road gets rough.

✓ Life will test you—but when you have **yourself and your "why,"** you have everything you need to thrive.

✓ **No matter how difficult the journey gets, your "why" will always remind you why you started.**

Chapter 14: Positivity – The Toppings That Make Life Sweeter

1. Self as the Foundation, "Why" as the Fuel, Positivity as the Topping

Building Your Life Recipe

Life is like a recipe—you need **a strong foundation, a driving force, and something that makes it enjoyable.**

✓ **Your foundation (yourself)** keeps you **grounded.**

✓ Your "why" **(your purpose)** drives you **forward.**

✓ **Positivity is the topping** that makes the journey **brighter, no matter how challenging it gets.**

Example:

- A cake needs a **solid base** to hold it together.
- It needs **ingredients that give it purpose**, like flour, eggs, and sugar.
- But what makes it **delightful**? The toppings—the icing, sprinkles, or whatever makes it special.

✓ **Positivity is that final ingredient**—it doesn't change what's underneath, but it makes the experience **sweeter, brighter, and more enjoyable.**

Why Positivity Matters

✓ **Life will never be perfect.** Challenges, disappointments, and struggles are inevitable.

✓ **But choosing to see the good gives you the strength to handle the bad.**

Example:

- A tough day **doesn't have to be a bad day** if you choose to focus on **small moments of joy.**
- You might have had a stressful meeting, but maybe you also had a **great conversation with a friend** or enjoyed your **favorite meal.**

✓ **Better mindset:**

"Even on my hardest days, there's something good if I choose to look for it."

2. Positivity is a Choice

Happiness Isn't Automatic

✓ **No one wakes up happy every day.**

✓ **Happiness is a decision you make, no matter what's happening around you.**

Some people **wait for happiness** to come to them.

✓ Others **create happiness** by choosing to **see the good.**

Example:
- You **don't have control** over every event in your life.
- But you **do have control** over **how you respond** to it.

✓ **Better mindset:**

"I can't control everything, but I can choose how I react."

Choosing Positivity Doesn't Mean Ignoring Problems

✓ **Positivity isn't pretending everything is perfect.**

✓ **It's about choosing to approach problems with hope and resilience.**

Example:

- Instead of saying, *"Everything is fine,"* when it's not...
- Say, *"This is tough, but I know I'll get through it."*

✓ **Better mindset:**

"I acknowledge my struggles, but I won't let them define my entire outlook."

Starting Your Day with Intention

Every morning, **decide** that you will carry **positivity with you—no matter what the day brings.**

✓ **Your mindset at the start of the day affects your entire experience.**

Affirmation   **Example:**

"Today, I choose to find the good in every situation."

✓ **Why it works:**

- A positive mindset **attracts positive experiences.**
- When you **train your mind to focus on the good,** you naturally create a better reality.

Positivity is a Skill You Build Daily

✓ **You don't have to ignore your struggles to be positive.**

✓ **You don't have to wait for happiness—you create it.**

✓ **Choosing positivity isn't about pretending—it's about believing in your ability to rise above challenges.**

Every day, you have the power to choose. Choose light. Choose hope. Choose growth.

3. How Positivity Changes Your Perspective

The Power of Focus

✓ **What you focus on grows.**

✓ When you focus on **the good,** you create more room for **joy, gratitude, and peace.**

Example:

- If you **fixate on what went wrong at work,** that's all you'll think about.
- But if you **choose to focus on what went right,** your entire day shifts.

Better mindset:

"Every situation has positives and negatives—I choose to focus on what helps me."

Reframing Challenges

✓ **Positivity doesn't deny difficulties—it transforms how you see them.**

Example:

- Instead of **"I failed,"** say, **"I learned something new."**
- Instead of **"This is impossible,"** say, **"I haven't figured it out yet."**

Better mindset:

"Every challenge is a lesson if I choose to see it that way."

Why This Shift Matters

✓ Your perspective shapes your reality.

✓ Seeing possibilities instead of roadblocks keeps you moving forward.

✓ A small shift in thinking can create a massive shift in your life.

You can't control every situation, but you can always control how you choose to see it.

4. Practical Ways to Choose Positivity

a. Start with Gratitude

Each morning, **write down or think of three things you're grateful for.**

Gratitude **shifts your focus to abundance instead of lack.**

Example:
- "I'm grateful for my health."
- "I'm grateful for my support system."
- "I'm grateful for the opportunity to grow today."

Better mindset:

"The more I appreciate, the more I attract good things into my life."

b. Find Small Joys Throughout the Day

Look for **little moments** that bring happiness.

Even **a kind word, a warm cup of coffee, or a beautiful sunset** can be uplifting.

Example:
- Instead of **waiting for something big to make you happy,** enjoy the **small moments.**

✓ **Better mindset:**

"Happiness is in the details of everyday life."

c. Practice Positive Self-Talk

Your **words shape your reality.**

Replace **negative thoughts with empowering ones.**

Example:
- Instead of **"I can't do this,"** say, **"I'll figure this out."**

✓ **Better mindset:**
"I am capable, strong, and always growing."

d. Surround Yourself with Positivity
Spend time with **people, activities, and environments** that uplift you.
If something **drains your energy, set boundaries.**

Example:
- Reduce time spent with **negative influences** and **increase time with things that inspire you.**

✓ **Better mindset:**
"I choose to be around people and experiences that bring out the best in me."

5. Positivity is a Habit, Not a Destination
Building the Positivity Muscle

Positivity isn't something you wake up with one day and suddenly have forever—it's a **habit that needs to be built over time.** Like exercising a muscle, the more you train your mind to **look for the good,** the stronger that mindset becomes.

✓ At first, it might feel unnatural or forced—especially if you're used to focusing on what's wrong.

✓ But with time, positivity becomes **your default mode,** and you start seeing life differently.

Example:

- If you **start every morning with one positive thought,** over time, it becomes second nature.
- You may not notice the shift immediately, but weeks or months later, you'll realize that **your perspective has changed.**

✓ **Better mindset:**

"Positivity isn't something I have—it's something I practice daily."

It's Okay to Have Off Days

Even the most positive people **have bad days.** The key is understanding that positivity **isn't about ignoring reality—it's about choosing how you engage with it.**

✓ Being positive doesn't mean **pretending everything is great when it's not.**

✓ It doesn't mean **denying your feelings or suppressing emotions.**

✓ It means **allowing yourself to feel, process, and then move forward without letting negativity take over.**

   Example:

- Maybe you wake up feeling drained and unmotivated. Instead of forcing yourself to **fake happiness,** allow yourself to acknowledge the feeling: *"I'm not feeling my best today, and that's okay."*
- The difference? Instead of getting stuck in that mood, you **find small ways to lift yourself up.**
- A walk outside.
- Listening to music you love.
- A reminder that tomorrow is a new day.

✓ **Better mindset:**

"I allow myself to feel, but I won't let negativity define me."

Why This Matters

✓ Just like you wouldn't expect to be physically fit after **one workout,** you can't expect to be positive all the time without practice.

✓ Some days, **positivity will come naturally.** Other days, it will feel like work—and that's okay.

✓ The goal isn't to be positive **100% of the time** but to build the **resilience to shift your mindset when you need to.**

The more you practice choosing light, the easier it becomes to find it—even on dark days.

6. Reflection Exercise: Choosing Positivity

This exercise is about **training your mind** to focus on the good, no matter how small. When you intentionally seek out positive moments, you start **rewiring your brain** to notice them more naturally.

At the Start of Your Day:
Write down one thing you're excited about.

It doesn't have to be something huge—just **one thing that sparks even a little joy.**

Example:
- "I'm excited to have my favorite coffee this morning."
- "I'm looking forward to listening to a new podcast on my way to work."
- "I'm excited to make progress on my personal goals today."

✓ **Why it works:**

- It shifts your focus **from dread to anticipation.**
- It reminds you that **even on routine days, there's something to look forward to.**

At the End of Your Day:
Write down one thing that made you smile.

Even on rough days, **there's always something small to appreciate.** Maybe a song you love played on the radio. Maybe a stranger held the door open for you. Maybe you had a peaceful moment to yourself.

Example:
- "A coworker complimented my work."
- "I saw a funny meme that made me laugh."
- "I got through a stressful day and still found time to take care of myself."

Why it works:
- Helps you **end your day on a positive note.**
- Reinforces the idea that **good things happen every day, even when things feel difficult.**

Reflect on How These Small Moments Impact Your Mood

What do you notice when you focus on the positives? What small habits make your day feel better?

Example:
- If you notice that **gratitude shifts your energy,** keep practicing it.
- If you realize that **a certain morning routine improves your mindset,** make it a habit.

Better mindset:

"Small shifts in focus can transform my entire outlook."

Why This Exercise Matters

✓ Happiness isn't just about big achievements—it's built in small, everyday moments.

✓ When you train yourself to find joy in the little things, your entire perspective on life changes.

✓ Positivity isn't something you find—it's something you create. The more you seek the good, the more good you'll find.

Closing the Chapter

Positivity is the **final ingredient** that makes life **meaningful and enjoyable.** It's what turns **ordinary moments into something special** and allows you to navigate challenges **without losing sight of the good.**

✓ Positivity isn't about pretending life is perfect—it's about choosing to focus on what's still beautiful, even in imperfection.

✓ It's about finding joy in small moments, strength in difficulties, and gratitude in everyday life.

✓ Every day, you have a choice: let life dictate your happiness, or take control and create it for yourself.

When you wake up every morning and decide to be happy, you're not just adding sweetness to your life—you're transforming it.

Chapter 15: The Age of Knowledge – Learning and Understanding in Modern Times

1. The Power of Knowledge in Your Hands

We Live in the Most Connected Time in History

There has never been a time in human history when knowledge has been more **accessible, instant, and limitless** than it is today.

✓ The **internet, AI, and digital learning platforms** have made it possible to learn almost anything **on demand**.

✓ With just a **few clicks**, you can access **expert insights, university courses, scientific research, and personal development resources.**

Example:

- In the past, if you wanted to learn a new language, you needed **formal classes or expensive textbooks**.
- Today, you can **download an app, join an online community, or even talk to native speakers instantly.**

✓ **Information is no longer hidden behind barriers—it's right at your fingertips.**

What This Means for You

Because we live in this **age of knowledge**, you have an **incredible advantage**—but only if you use it wisely.

✓ If you want to **learn a skill, understand a complex topic, or expand your mind,** you don't have to wait for someone to teach you.

✓ The tools to **educate yourself, grow, and evolve** are more accessible than ever.

Example:

- If you're interested in **starting a business**, you can find **free courses, expert advice, and successful entrepreneurs** sharing their experiences—all online.
- If you want to **improve your health**, you can **research diets, watch workout videos, or join fitness communities.**

✓ **The only limit is how much effort you put into learning and applying what you discover.**

2. The Abundance of Information

A Double-Edged Sword

The internet has given us access to **more knowledge than ever before**, but with that comes a major challenge:

✓ **There's TOO MUCH information.**

✓ **Not everything is useful, accurate, or credible.**

✓ **Overconsumption can lead to confusion, inaction, or even misinformation.**

Example:

- If you search for **"best diet for health,"** you'll find thousands of conflicting opinions:
- One expert says **low-carb** is best.
- Another swears by **veganism.**
- Someone else claims **intermittent fasting** is the key.

Without discernment, you can end up trapped in information overload instead of actually taking action.

✓ **The challenge is no longer FINDING knowledge—it's learning how to FILTER what's useful.**

Using Knowledge With Discernment

✓ Not everything you read, watch, or hear is true or valuable.

✓ Developing critical thinking is essential in today's world.

   Example:

- If you're researching a topic, **don't rely on just one source.**
- Instead of blindly trusting the first thing you read, **compare different perspectives.**
- Look at **scientific research.**
- Consider **expert opinions.**
- Seek **real-world experiences.**

   Better mindset:

"I don't just absorb information—I question, analyze, and verify before accepting it."

Why This Matters

✓ Having access to unlimited knowledge is useless if you don't know how to filter truth from noise.

✓ Blindly accepting everything leads to misinformation and confusion.

✓ When you develop discernment, you gain control over what truly shapes your beliefs and decisions.

   Knowledge is power, but only if you know how to use it wisely.

3. Tools for Learning and Growth

Modern Tools for Personal Development

   In the past, **learning required formal education, expensive courses, and physical books.**

Today, **you can learn almost anything for free or at a low cost**—right from your phone or computer.

Learning tool examples:

Online courses – *Coursera, Udemy, Skillshare, YouTube*

Research tools – *Google Scholar, PubMed, AI tools like ChatGPT*

Community platforms – *Reddit, Quora, niche forums*

Example:

- Want to learn **coding?** You can start for **free** on **Codecademy** or **freeCodeCamp.**

- Want to study **psychology, marketing, or finance?** Ivy League schools offer free courses on **Coursera.**

- Curious about **health and wellness?** You can read actual **scientific studies** on **PubMed.**

✓ **There are no excuses—the resources are there.** The real question is:

"Are you willing to use them?"

How to Use These Tools Effectively

✓ **Set a clear goal before diving into learning.**

✓ **Break down complex topics into manageable steps.**

✓ **Apply what you learn—don't just consume knowledge passively.**

Example:

- Instead of **binge-watching self-improvement videos,** pick one lesson and **actually apply it.**

- If you're **learning a new skill,** practice it **daily** instead of just **reading about it.**

Better mindset:

"Knowledge without action is just entertainment. Make it count."

Why This Matters

✓ We live in an era where information is limitless—what you do with it is up to you.

✓ There's never been an easier time to gain new skills, shift careers, or improve yourself.

✓ Learning is no longer about access—it's about initiative.

Your next breakthrough is one decision away. The tools are waiting. Are you ready to use them?

4. The Democratization of Learning

Accessible to All

There was a time when **knowledge was reserved for the wealthy, the privileged, or those with access to elite institutions.** Today, **that barrier is gone.**

✓ **If you have an internet connection,** you have access to the **same knowledge** as Ivy League students, top industry leaders, and experts in any field.

✓ **Education is no longer locked behind institutions**—it's available to anyone who seeks it.

Example:

- A student in a **remote village** can take the same **Harvard and MIT courses online** as someone sitting in a university classroom.

- **Entrepreneurs without formal business degrees** can learn marketing, finance, and leadership **for free** through online courses and mentorship communities.

- **Self-taught developers, designers, and writers** are building careers **without ever stepping into a classroom.**

✓ **The playing field is more level than ever—what you do with this opportunity is up to you.**

How to Take Advantage of This Opportunity

✓ **Explore free resources:** *TED Talks, Khan Academy, Project Gutenberg (for free books), EdX, Open Yale Courses.*

✓ **Join virtual communities:** *Engage in online discussions, collaborate on projects, and learn from others through Reddit, Discord groups, or LinkedIn forums.*

✓ **Commit to lifelong learning:** *The world is evolving fast—those who stay curious and adaptable will always be ahead.*

   Example:

- Instead of **scrolling mindlessly on social media,** spend **10 minutes a day learning something new.**
- Turn passive time (like commuting) into learning time— **listen to podcasts, audiobooks, or expert talks.**
- Make **reading, watching educational content, or engaging with industry leaders** part of your daily habits.

   Better mindset:

"What I choose to learn today shapes my future."

Why This Matters

✓ **No excuses—opportunity is everywhere.**

✓ **Your access to knowledge is unlimited—the only limit is your willingness to learn.**

✓ In a world where information is free, ignorance is a choice. The future belongs to those who never stop learning.

5. How to Balance Learning With Action

Knowledge Alone Isn't Enough

✓ Learning is valuable, but real understanding comes from APPLYING what you've learned.

✓ Absorbing information without action is like collecting tools but never using them.

Example:

- Watching a video on **mindfulness** is great—but actually **practicing mindfulness daily** is what makes a difference.

- Reading books about **fitness and nutrition** won't improve your health—**exercising and eating well will.**

- Learning **about** success won't bring success—you need to **take steps toward it.**

✓ **Better mindset:**

"I don't just learn—I apply, experiment, and grow."

Avoiding Overconsumption

✓ Many people **get stuck in "learning mode"** without ever taking action.

✓ They **keep reading, watching, and researching**—but never actually DO anything.

Example:

- You've read **10 books on starting a business** but haven't taken a single step toward launching one.

- You've watched **countless tutorials on a skill** but never practiced it yourself.
- You **plan and plan**, waiting for the "perfect" time—but **never actually start.**

Better mindset:

"Knowledge is potential—action is power."

How to Shift From Learning to Action

✓ Set a deadline for when you'll start applying what you've learned.

✓ For every book you read, implement at least one lesson.

✓ Balance learning with doing—apply new skills in real life instead of just reading about them.

Example:

- Instead of **reading another self-improvement book,** pick one thing you've learned and start practicing it.
- Instead of **watching another fitness video,** do the workout.
- Instead of **studying entrepreneurship,** take one step—buy the domain, test an idea, or start small.

Why This Matters

✓ Information without action is just entertainment.

✓ Real progress happens when you take what you've learned and put it to use.

✓ Don't just be a consumer of knowledge—be a creator of change.

Learning is powerful, but action is what transforms your life.

6. Reflection Exercise: Leveraging Modern Knowledge

This exercise is designed to **help you bridge the gap** between learning and action.

a. Identify One Topic or Skill You've Been Wanting to Learn

Think about something **you've been interested in but haven't taken action on yet.**

✓ Is it **a new language?**

✓ Do you want to **improve a skill like writing, coding, or cooking?**

✓ Are you curious about **finance, psychology, or self-improvement?**

> **Example:**
> - *"I've always wanted to learn public speaking."*
> - *"I want to understand how to invest in stocks."*
> - *"I need to improve my writing skills."*

b. Research 2-3 Resources You Can Use to Explore That Topic

Look for **credible and actionable** sources:

✓ **Books** – Find expert-backed books on your chosen topic.

✓ **Online Courses** – Coursera, Udemy, YouTube, or Khan Academy.

✓ **Podcasts or Blogs** – Learn from professionals sharing real-world insights.

> **Example:**
> - If you want to **learn public speaking**, find **TED Talks, Toastmasters, or courses on effective communication.**

- If you're interested in **investing**, explore **books like *The Intelligent Investor*, online stock courses, or financial podcasts.**
- If you want to **improve writing**, check out **Grammarly, writing masterclasses, or daily journaling exercises.**

c. Set a Goal for How You'll Apply What You Learn in the Next Week or Month

✓ **Learning without action doesn't lead to growth.**

✓ Set a **clear, measurable goal** to **apply what you've learned.**

Example:

- If you want to **improve public speaking**, commit to **recording yourself speaking for 5 minutes every day.**
- If you want to **learn about investing**, read **one book and apply one investment principle.**
- If you want to **write better**, challenge yourself to **write 500 words daily for a month.**

✓ **The key is to turn knowledge into action.**

Why This Matters

✓ This reflection helps you go from just thinking about learning to actually doing something with it.

✓ It forces you to take the first step—because the hardest part of any new skill is starting.

✓ The world's knowledge is at your fingertips. What you do with it is up to you.

The future belongs to those who take action—starting now.

Closing the Chapter

✔ We live in a time where knowledge is abundant, accessible, and limitless.

✔ The tools to grow, learn, and evolve are right at your fingertips— but what you do with them is up to you.

✔ You no longer have to wait for permission to gain knowledge, build skills, or change your life.

The key is not just to consume knowledge, but to apply it.

Chapter 16: Tips and Tricks to Get Along with Others

Relationships—whether personal or professional—are built on connection. But getting along with people isn't always about deep conversations or shared values.

Sometimes, the secret to building rapport lies in subtle, almost invisible actions—the way you make people feel at ease, understood, and appreciated.

This chapter is your toolkit for creating effortless, genuine connections with anyone—whether it's:

✓ A new friend.

✓ A coworker.

✓ Someone you just met at a social event.

What This Chapter Is About:

✓ Understanding human nature.

✓ Respecting differences.

✓ Making interactions feel natural and enjoyable.

These techniques aren't about manipulation or pretending to be someone you're not. They're about learning how to navigate social dynamics in a way that feels authentic and effortless.

Because when you understand how people work, getting along with them becomes second nature.

1. The Power of Mirroring

Mirroring is the **art of subtly mimicking** someone's **body language, tone, and speech patterns** to create an **unspoken bond.**

✓ It's something we **naturally do** when we feel comfortable with someone.

✓ But when used **intentionally and subtly**, it can **fast-track rapport** and help people feel **more connected to you.**

How to Mirror Effectively:
Body Language:

If someone **leans forward while speaking**, lean slightly forward too.

If they **gesture with their hands**, use similar, natural gestures. If they sit with their **arms relaxed**, avoid crossing yours (crossed arms can signal defensiveness).

Example:

- If someone is **sitting back, relaxed, and smiling**, mirroring that posture creates an **instant sense of ease.**

- If they **nod while talking**, a subtle nod in return shows **engagement and agreement.**

Tone and Speech:

Match their **tone and pace**—if they're **calm and soft-spoken,** slow your pace. If they're **excited and expressive,** match their enthusiasm.

Subtly repeat **key phrases** they use, weaving them into your responses.

Example:

- If someone says, *"I had such a stressful week,"* instead of **immediately jumping to your own story**, mirror their **words and emotion**:

"Ugh, that sounds exhausting. What happened?"

- If someone often says *"That's crazy!"* or *"Oh wow, really?"*—using those phrases **naturally** in conversation **subconsciously builds familiarity.**

Why It Works:

People are naturally drawn to those who reflect their behavior—it signals **safety and understanding.**

When done subtly, mirroring makes people feel heard, seen, and comfortable around you.

It helps **build trust faster** because the person **feels understood on a subconscious level.**

Warning: Don't make it too obvious or robotic—it should feel natural, not forced.

- If you **copy everything exactly**, it can come off as **awkward or even creepy.**
- The goal is to **enhance connection**, not mimic **like a mirror image.**

When to Use Mirroring:

✓ In **job interviews** to create **rapport with an interviewer.**

✓ On **first dates** to make conversations **flow naturally.**

✓ In **business meetings** to **establish trust and cooperation.**

✓ In **everyday interactions** to make people **feel more comfortable and open with you.**

Mirroring is a subtle yet powerful way to make people feel at ease—without saying a word.

2. Find Common Ground

People bond over **similarities**—even the smallest shared experiences can create an **instant connection.**

✓ **We naturally feel more comfortable around people who remind us of ourselves.**

✓ **Finding common ground makes conversations flow easily and reduces social tension.**

✓ **How to Do It:**

Ask Open-Ended Questions

The easiest way to **find something in common** is to ask questions that encourage people to **share about themselves.**

Examples:

- *"What do you like to do for fun?"*
- *"Where did you grow up?"*
- *"What's your favorite [movie, food, place to visit]?"*
- *"What's something you've been really into lately?"*

Why this works:

✓ Open-ended questions **invite longer, more natural conversations** (instead of just yes/no answers).

✓ They allow the other person to **share something personal**, which helps you find **common ground faster.**

Look for Shared Experiences

Once they mention **a hobby, interest, or experience**, look for a way to **connect with it.**

Example:

- **Them:** *"I love hiking."*
- **You:** *"Me too! Do you have a favorite trail?"*
- **Them:** *"I just started watching that Netflix show."*
- **You:** *"Oh, I saw the first season! What do you think so far?"*

✓ This keeps the conversation flowing without feeling forced.

✓ People feel more engaged when they talk about things they enjoy.

Highlight Shared Goals

Even if you don't have the same hobbies, you can **still find commonality in shared goals or situations.**

Example:

- *"We're both working on improving this project—it's great having someone like you who's equally committed."*
- *"I can totally relate! I'm also trying to be more consistent with working out."*

✓ This creates a "same team" mindset, making people feel like you're working together instead of just talking.

Why It Works:

- **Common ground creates a sense of belonging**—it reminds the other person that you're **on the same wavelength.**
- **It reduces tension and builds trust**—people naturally feel safer and more at ease around those who **understand them.**

- It makes conversations effortless—instead of struggling for topics, you have a **natural flow of discussion.**

Finding common ground isn't about pretending to be the same—it's about connecting through shared experiences, no matter how small.

Why Common Ground Matters

Wouldn't you feel **more comfortable talking to a stranger** about something **familiar** rather than something completely **outside your ballpark?**

Familiarity builds comfort.

✓ **It reduces the social barrier** that comes with meeting someone new.

✓ **It makes interactions feel effortless** instead of forced or awkward.

Example:

- If you meet someone at a party and they start talking about **quantum physics**, but you know nothing about it, the conversation might feel intimidating.
- But if they mention **a show you both love**, suddenly, there's a comfortable entry point for connection.

How Teachers Use Common Ground

Even in **education**, finding common ground **helps build trust and engagement.**

Example:

- Most teachers **introduce themselves** and get to know their students on the first day **before jumping into lessons.**
- Why? Because a teacher who understands their students **can teach more effectively.**

If a teacher and their students are **fans of the same show, movie, or game,** they can **use that as an example** to explain new concepts.

Example in the Classroom:

- A math teacher might say:

  "You know how in basketball, players use angles to make a perfect shot? Geometry works the same way!"

- A history teacher might relate a topic to something modern:

  "The way ancient empires expanded is a lot like how major tech companies compete for dominance today."

Why this works:

It makes the subject **more relatable and less intimidating.**

It **builds engagement** because students are learning through something they **already understand.**

It helps people feel like they're **learning from someone who gets them.**

Applying This to Everyday Conversations

✓ Finding common ground isn't just about comfort—it's about creating a foundation for deeper connections.

✓ Whether you're meeting a new coworker, networking, or even dating, common interests break the ice.

✓ People are more open to learning new things when they first feel understood.

The easiest way to connect with someone isn't by impressing them—it's by relating to them.

3. Active Listening: Go Beyond Words

We've already talked about **active listening**, but let's take it a step further.

The goal isn't just to hear people—it's to make them feel truly understood.

When you listen **on a deeper level**, people naturally **trust you more,** feel **closer to you,** and enjoy conversations with you.

Advanced Active Listening Techniques:

a. Nod and Respond

- Use **subtle, encouraging gestures** to show engagement.
- A simple **nod, smile, or verbal acknowledgment** (like *"That makes sense"* or *"Wow, really?"*) signals that you're paying attention.

Example:

- **Them:** *"I've been working really hard on this new project."*
- **You:** *(Nods)* *"That sounds exciting! What's been the most rewarding part so far?"*

Why this works:

It reassures the speaker that **you're following along.** It **keeps the conversation flowing naturally** without awkward pauses.

b. Ask Follow-Up Questions

- Instead of just responding with *"Oh, that's cool"*, ask **open-ended questions** that encourage them to share more.
- This **deepens the conversation** and makes the other person feel valued.

Examples:
- If they mention a trip:
  "That sounds amazing! What was your favorite part?"
- If they share a challenge:
  "That must've been tough. How did you handle it?"
- If they talk about a new hobby:
  "That's interesting! What got you into that?"

Why this works:
- **Shows that you're genuinely interested** in them.
- **Encourages them to open up**, which builds **deeper connections**.
- **People love talking to those who make them feel important.**

c. Show Genuine Interest
- People can always **tell the difference** between someone who's actually listening and someone who's just **waiting for their turn to talk.**
- Focus on **what they're saying, not just how you'll respond.**

Example:
- If someone shares a personal story, resist the urge to **immediately relate it to yourself.**

- Instead of *"Oh yeah, that happened to me too,"* try **staying on their experience first**:

  "That must've been a big moment for you. What did you take away from it?"

Why this works:

It **shifts the focus to them,** which makes them feel valued.

It **shows that you're not just waiting to speak—you're actually engaged.**

It makes people feel **seen, heard, and understood.**

Why Advanced Active Listening Works:

- **It deepens trust**—when people feel truly heard, they **open up more.**
- **It creates emotional connection**—people will naturally feel **closer to you.**
- **It makes you a person others enjoy talking to**—which strengthens friendships, work relationships, and even first impressions.

People may forget what you said, but they'll never forget how you made them feel.

4. Use Positive Body Language

Your **body speaks before your words do**—people pick up on **nonverbal cues** before they even hear what you say.

✓ If your body language **contradicts** your words, people will trust what they **see** over what they hear.

✓ If you want to create **warmth, openness, and connection**, your **nonverbal cues must align with your intention.**

How to Show Open and Warm Body Language:

a. Smile Genuinely

- A **real** smile instantly makes you **approachable and welcoming.**
- People are naturally **drawn to warmth**, and smiling sets a **positive tone** for the conversation.

Example:

- If you're meeting someone new, a **simple, genuine smile** makes you **seem friendly and inviting.**
- If you're in a group setting, **smiling when someone speaks** makes them feel **acknowledged and heard.**

b. Maintain Eye Contact

- **Not too much** (so you don't seem intense), but enough to **show engagement.**
- Eye contact builds **trust**—it signals that you're **fully present in the conversation.**

Tip:

- In **casual conversations**, aim for **eye contact about 60-70% of the time.**
- If direct eye contact feels **too intense**, look at their **nose or eyebrows** instead—it has the same effect.

c. Relax Your Posture

- Avoid crossing your arms or looking **tense**—this can make you **seem closed off.**
- Keep your shoulders relaxed and your posture **open.**

Example:

- **Closed posture:** Arms crossed, leaning away, stiff shoulders = Unapproachable.
- **Open posture:** Arms at your sides, leaning slightly forward, relaxed shoulders = Welcoming.

Why it matters:
- Even if you're **not feeling nervous**, crossed arms or stiff posture can **subconsciously** make people feel like you're **disinterested or defensive.**

d. Face Them Fully
- Angle your body toward the person to **signal your full attention.**
- If you're turned away or half-facing them, it can seem like **you're not fully engaged.**

Example:
- If you're in a **group conversation**, facing the person speaking shows **you're engaged.**
- If someone is talking to you **but your body is turned toward your phone or another direction**, it signals **disinterest.**

Why It Works:
- **People respond to warmth and openness**—your body language **sets the tone** for how they feel in your presence.
- **Good body language makes conversations smoother and more enjoyable.**
- **It creates an inviting space where people feel comfortable opening up to you.**

Before you even say a word, your body has already spoken. Make sure it's saying the right thing.

5. Give Compliments (But Make Them Specific)

Everyone loves a compliment—but **generic ones can feel shallow or insincere.**

✓ **A well-placed, specific compliment makes people feel genuinely valued and appreciated.**

How to Give Meaningful Compliments:
- Make it about something unique to them.
- Point out a specific trait, skill, or action.
- Show that you're truly paying attention.

Example:
- **Generic compliment:** *"You're so smart."*
- **Better compliment:** *"The way you explained that was so clear and insightful—I wouldn't have thought of it that way."*

More Examples:

✓ *"I admire how you handled that situation earlier. You stayed so calm under pressure."*

✓ *"You've got a great sense of humor—it's so refreshing."*

✓ *"I love how passionate you are when you talk about things that matter to you."*

✓ *"You always make people feel comfortable—you have such a welcoming energy."*

Why It Works:

- **Specific compliments feel authentic**—they show you're not just saying something to be nice, but that you truly noticed and appreciated them.
- **They make people feel seen**—instead of a vague compliment, they know **exactly what they did well.**
- **They deepen connections**—people remember those who genuinely appreciate them.

The best compliments aren't just about flattery—they're about making someone feel valued.

6. Ask for Their Opinions

People **love feeling valued.** Asking for someone's **opinion or perspective** makes them feel **respected and appreciated.**

✓ It shows that you **trust their judgment.**

✓ It gives them a chance to **share their thoughts in a meaningful way.**

✓ It helps **build stronger connections** by making conversations more **engaging and collaborative.**

Examples of How to Ask for Opinions:
General Conversations:
- *"What do you think about this idea?"*
- *"I'd love to hear your take on this."*
- *"What's your perspective on this situation?"*

Work & Decision-Making:
- *"How would you approach this challenge?"*

- *"I really respect your expertise—what's your opinion on this?"*
- *"If you were in my position, how would you handle this?"*

Personal & Social Situations:
- *"Which option do you think is better? I trust your judgment."*
- *"I'm thinking about trying something new—what do you think?"*
- *"What's your honest opinion on this? I value your input."*

Why It Works:
- **People feel important** when their thoughts and insights are valued.
- **It creates mutual respect**—showing that you **see them as someone worth learning from.**
- **It strengthens relationships** by making conversations **more balanced and engaging.**
- **It makes people feel heard and appreciated**, which naturally makes them enjoy your presence more.

The easiest way to make someone feel important? Genuinely value their thoughts.

Side Note: The Power of Simple Conversation Starters
Sometimes, **the simplest approach is the most effective.**

One of the **most successful pickup lines** I've ever observed was:

✓ A guy asking a girl **what she's drinking** and then **complimenting her drink**, saying that it looked good.

Example:

- *"That looks really good—what are you drinking?"*
- *"That's an interesting cocktail. Do you recommend it?"*

Why it works:
- **It's casual and non-threatening**—it doesn't put pressure on the conversation.
- **It immediately finds common ground**—since they're both at the same place, they already have shared context.
- **It invites the other person to talk**—people usually love sharing their preferences.
- **It feels natural**—unlike rehearsed pickup lines, this feels like a simple, genuine interaction.

Takeaway:
Sometimes, **a little can go a long way.** The best way to start a conversation **isn't about impressing someone—it's about creating an easy, natural moment of connection.**

7. Be Mindful of Their Energy

Every **interaction has an energy to it.**

✓ Some people **love high-energy conversations** and feed off excitement.

✓ Others **prefer a calmer, more thoughtful approach** and don't enjoy being overwhelmed.

Being **aware of someone's energy** and adjusting accordingly makes your interactions **feel effortless, natural, and enjoyable.**

How to Adapt:
Match Their Energy (Without Imitating)

213

- If they're **animated and expressive**, reflect that **enthusiasm and playfulness** back.
- If they're **reserved and soft-spoken**, **slow your pace** and let them set the rhythm.

  Example:
- Talking to an **excited extrovert?** Keep the **momentum going** with engaging, upbeat responses.
- Chatting with someone **quiet and introspective?** Give them space to **think and process before jumping in.**

✓ **The key is to mirror their comfort level—not force a different energy onto them.**

Pay Attention to Cues

People **give nonverbal signs** about their energy levels, even if they don't say anything directly.

Examples of cues to watch for:
- **If they seem distracted or tired** → Don't overwhelm them with **rapid-fire questions**—give them room to breathe.
- **If they keep checking their phone or looking around** → They may not be fully present—adjust by keeping the conversation light.
- **If they're giving long, detailed responses** → They're engaged—feel free to match that with enthusiasm and depth.

✓ **When you're mindful of someone's state of mind, you create a space where they feel comfortable.**

Why It Works:

Adapting to someone's energy makes interactions feel effortless—you're working *with* their vibe, not against it. People naturally feel more at ease when conversations move at a pace that feels comfortable for them. It shows social awareness and emotional intelligence, making you someone people *enjoy* talking to.

The best connections happen when you meet people where they are—not where you expect them to be.

8. Be Authentic

People can sense when someone is being fake.
✓ Trying too hard to impress, act perfect, or fit in often has the opposite effect—it creates distance instead of connection.
✓ Authenticity makes people feel safe, understood, and drawn to you naturally.

How to Be Authentic:
a. Don't Try to Impress—Just Be Yourself

- You don't need to be the funniest, smartest, or most interesting person in the room to make an impact.
- Instead of trying to say the "right" thing, just say what feels natural to you.

Example:

- If someone talks about a topic you don't know much about, instead of pretending, say: *"I don't know much about that, but I'd love to hear more."*
- If someone asks your opinion on something you don't agree with, instead of forcing fake agreement, say:

215

"I see why you think that! My perspective is a little different, but I respect where you're coming from."

Why it works:

- Honesty makes you more relatable.
- You don't need to be perfect—you just need to be real.

b. Share Your Own Experiences & Vulnerabilities (When Appropriate)

- Being **real** means **not pretending to have everything figured out.**
- People connect with **stories, struggles, and shared experiences** more than perfection.

   Example:

- If someone talks about **a personal challenge**, instead of giving generic advice, you could say: *"I went through something similar, and it was really tough. Here's what helped me."*

Why it works:

- Openness builds trust.
- It reminds people they're not alone in their experiences.

c. Focus on Connecting, Not Performing

- Instead of **worrying about being "likable"**, focus on **genuinely engaging with others.**

- You don't need to **always be funny, always be interesting, or always be agreeable**—just be **present**.

  Example:
- Instead of thinking, *"How can I impress them?"*, shift to *"How can I enjoy this conversation?"*

Why It Works:
- **When you're real, people feel they can trust you.**
- **Authenticity creates deeper, more meaningful connections.**
- **People remember those who made them feel seen, not those who tried the hardest to impress them.**

The easiest way to get along with people? **Just be yourself—**because that's what people truly connect with.

Reflection Exercise: Strengthening Your Connections

This exercise will help you **apply what you've learned** and improve your interactions **in real life.**

a. Think of a Relationship or Interaction You'd Like to Improve
- Is it a **friendship that feels distant?**
- A **coworker you struggle to connect with?**
- Someone **new you'd like to build rapport with?**

  Example:
- *"I want to get along better with my coworker so we can collaborate more easily."*
- *"I'd like to strengthen my bond with a friend I haven't connected with in a while."*

- *"I want to feel more comfortable in social settings and make conversations flow better."*

b. Which Tips From This Chapter Can You Apply?

Review the techniques from this chapter and **choose one or more** that could improve the situation.

Examples:

- **Mirroring:** *"I'll subtly match their body language and tone to create a natural connection."*

- **Finding Common Ground:** *"I'll ask more open-ended questions to discover shared interests."*

- **Active Listening:** *"I'll focus on making them feel heard instead of thinking about my next response."*

- **Being Mindful of Their Energy:** *"I'll adjust my approach based on their level of enthusiasm or reserve."*

c. After Trying One or More Techniques, Reflect on the Results

✔ **How did the other person respond?**

Did they seem more engaged?

Did they open up more than usual?

Did the conversation feel smoother or more natural?

✔ **How did it feel to intentionally create connection?**

Did you feel more confident?

Did the interaction feel easier and more enjoyable?

What surprised you about the outcome?

Why This Matters:

✓ The **best way to improve social skills** is through **intentional practice.**

✓ **Small changes in communication** can lead to **major improvements** in relationships.

✓ **The more you apply these techniques, the more natural they'll become.**

Meaningful connections don't happen by accident—they're built through small, intentional actions.

Final Thoughts: The Art of Connection

✓ Getting along with people isn't about being perfect—it's about being present, curious, and empathetic.

✓ **Small, intentional actions**—like listening actively, adapting to their energy, and finding common ground—can turn even the most casual interactions into **genuine, meaningful connections.**

✓ **People don't remember every word you say, but they always remember how you made them feel.**

Chapter 17: Building Self-Confidence

Confidence **doesn't come naturally** to everyone—but here's the good news:

✓ **Confidence is a skill, not a fixed trait.**

✓ **It's something you can build, strengthen, and refine over time.**

✓ **Like any skill, it grows with practice, intention, and consistency.**

The Truth About Confidence:

Some people **seem naturally confident**, but in reality, confidence isn't something you're **born with—it's something you develop.**

True confidence **isn't about never feeling nervous, uncertain, or afraid**—it's about **trusting yourself to handle whatever comes your way.**

It's not about **always knowing the right answer**—it's about believing that, even if you don't, **you'll figure it out.**

Confidence isn't about being perfect—it's about showing up, trusting yourself, and taking up space.

1. Fake It Till You Make It

The phrase might sound cliché, but **it works.**

✓ **Confidence doesn't always start with feeling confident**—sometimes, it starts with **acting confident until your mind and body catch up.**

Why It Works:

Your brain follows your body's lead.

- When you **stand tall, speak clearly, and project confidence**, your mind starts believing it's true.

People respond to confidence.

- The more you **project** confidence, the more others will **treat you as confident**—which reinforces the feeling.

Momentum builds.

- The more you **act confidently**, the more real confidence **develops over time.**

How to Fake It:

Posture & Body Language

- **Stand tall**—shoulders back, chin up.
- **Avoid closed-off body language**—don't cross your arms or look down.
- **Walk into a room as if you belong there.**

Why?

✓ Confident body language **immediately shifts your mindset.**

✓ You **look and feel more self-assured**, even if you're still nervous inside.

Speak With Intention

- **Use a clear, steady tone.**
- **If you feel nervous, slow down and pause**—rushing makes you sound unsure.
- **When you slow down and pause, you send a subconscious message that you take the time to think things through first and are not impulsive.**

✓ Speaking **deliberately** gives your words **more weight and impact.**

Smile

A **genuine smile** makes you look **approachable and self-assured.**

Smiling also **tricks your brain into feeling more positive**—it's scientifically proven!

Example:

Imagine you're **nervous about speaking in a meeting.**

✓ Instead of **letting anxiety take over,**

✓ **Sit up straight, take a deep breath, and speak as though you're already confident.**

Over time, acting confident turns into real confidence.

✓ **Confidence isn't about never feeling nervous—it's about moving forward despite it.**

2. Dress for Success—But Stay Comfortable

✓ **What you wear can have a huge impact on your confidence. It's not about expensive clothes or following trends—it's about wearing what makes you feel like your best self.**

The right outfit **doesn't just change how others see you—it changes how you see yourself.**

Tips for Dressing Confidently:
Wear Outfits That Empower You

- Choose clothes that make you feel **capable, stylish, and put together.**

- If you feel **powerful in a structured blazer, sleek in all black, or bold in bright colors—lean into that.**
  Why?

✓ When you wear **something that makes you feel strong**, you naturally **carry yourself with more confidence.**

Choose Colors or Styles That Match Your Energy
- Bright colors can **boost your mood** and make you feel more outgoing.
- Neutrals and darker tones can **make you feel sleek, confident, and in control.**
- Soft, comfortable textures can **help with calmness and ease.**
  Example:
- A bold red dress or power suit can make you feel **commanding and fearless.**
- A tailored black outfit can make you feel **effortlessly stylish and sophisticated.**
- A cozy, well-fitted sweater might help you feel **relaxed yet put-together.**

✓ **Color and style aren't just fashion choices—they affect how you feel.**

Prioritize Comfort
- **If you're uncomfortable, it shows.**
- Confidence comes from **feeling at ease in what you wear**, not from trying to squeeze into something that doesn't fit your body or personality.

- Clothes should **enhance** your confidence, not distract you from it.

Example:

- If you're constantly adjusting your clothes, **you won't be focused on the moment—you'll be focused on discomfort.**
- Wearing **shoes that hurt, pants that dig in, or outfits that don't feel "you"** will only make you self-conscious.

✓ **Confidence isn't about what you wear—it's about how you feel in what you wear.**

Reflection Question:
Think of a time you wore something that made you feel **powerful, stylish, or completely yourself.**

✓ **How did it change the way you carried yourself?**

✓ **How did people respond to you differently?**

Your outfit doesn't define you—but feeling good in your skin makes all the difference.

3. Be Prepared

✓ **Preparation is one of the most underrated keys to confidence.**

✓ **When you know you've done the work, you walk into any situation with a sense of control and readiness.**

Think about how much calmer and more confident you feel when you're prepared for something important.

- A **big meeting, an exam, a social event, or even just your daily routine**—when you're prepared, you naturally feel **more in control and less anxious.**

How to Prepare for Success:

a. Get a Full Night's Sleep

- Sleep fuels **your energy, focus, and mood.**
- A **solid night of rest before an important day** can make all the difference in how you carry yourself.
- Lack of sleep leads to **mental fog, irritability, and second-guessing yourself.**

Example:

- Compare how you feel after **8 hours of sleep** vs. running on **4 hours**—your ability to handle stress and make decisions is completely different.

✓ **A well-rested mind is a confident mind.**

b. Practice or Rehearse

- **Confidence comes from familiarity.**
- If you have a **presentation, interview, or big event**, practice **in front of a mirror, record yourself, or rehearse with a friend.**
- The more **you repeat something,** the **less intimidating it becomes.**

Example:

- **Public speaking feels scary**—but if you've **practiced multiple times**, it feels **manageable and even empowering.**
- **Social anxiety?** Practicing small talk **in your head** or writing out conversation starters can **help ease nervousness.**

✓ **The more you practice, the less fear has control over you.**

c. Plan Ahead

- **A little planning removes unnecessary stress.**
- Organizing **your outfit, schedule, and materials** in advance **prevents last-minute chaos.**
- When you're one step ahead, **you feel more in control and ready for the day.**

Example:

- **Think about the difference** between walking into a test **you studied for** vs. one **you didn't.**
- Walking into an important meeting **knowing your key points** vs. **winging it at the last minute.**

✓ **Preparation eliminates fear of the unknown and makes you feel in control.**

Why It Works:

When you're prepared, confidence follows naturally. Your brain doesn't have to scramble for answers—you've already set yourself up for success. Preparation replaces anxiety with certainty.

4. Prove to Yourself You Can

✓ **Confidence grows when you prove to yourself, over and over, that you're capable of achieving small wins.**

✓ **Even tiny accomplishments remind you of your potential.**

Confidence isn't built by waiting to feel ready—it's built through action.

- Every time you **push through doubt and succeed,** you teach yourself that **you're capable.**

- The **more proof you collect, the stronger your self-belief becomes.**

Ways to Prove Your Capabilities:
a. Learn Something New
- **Growth fuels confidence.**
- Whether it's **mastering a new skill, learning about a topic, or solving a problem**, even small accomplishments remind you that **you are improving.**

  Example:
- **Teaching yourself how to cook a new recipe.**
- **Figuring out a tech problem on your own.**
- **Picking up a new language or hobby.**

  ✓ **Every new thing you learn is proof that you are capable of growth.**

Take Baby Steps
- **Confidence isn't about massive leaps—it's about small, consistent progress.**
- Break big goals into **smaller, manageable tasks.**
- Each task you complete **is a win that builds momentum.**

  Example:
- Instead of saying, *"I want to get in shape,"* start with: *"I'll take a 10-minute walk every day."*
- Instead of saying, *"I want to be more social,"* start with: *"I'll initiate one conversation today."*

  ✓ **Each tiny win adds up to real, lasting confidence.**

c. Step Outside Your Comfort Zone

- **Fear shrinks when you face it.**
- Trying new things—even if they scare you—**reinforces that you're stronger and more capable than you think.**
- The more you do **things that challenge you**, the more **confident you become in your ability to handle anything.**

Example:

- **Speaking up in a meeting when you normally stay quiet.**
- **Saying yes to an opportunity that intimidates you.**
- **Traveling alone, trying a new activity, or meeting new people.**

✓ **Each time you challenge yourself, you prove that you are capable.**

Reflection:

Think of a time when you:

- Pushed through doubt and succeeded.
- Stepped outside your comfort zone and grew from it.
- Achieved something—even if it was small—and felt proud.

Confidence isn't given—it's built, one small win at a time.

5. Knowledge is Power

✓ **One of the quickest ways to feel confident is to know your stuff.**

✓ **When you've taken the time to educate yourself, you walk into any situation feeling informed and prepared.**

Confidence isn't about knowing everything—it's about knowing enough to navigate situations with ease.

How to Leverage Knowledge:
Read Up on Subjects
- The more **you know about a topic**, the **less intimidating conversations and decisions feel.**
- **Being well-informed gives you a sense of mastery and self-assurance.**

  Example:
- Walking into a meeting **knowing the key points** makes you feel **more confident about speaking up.**
- Knowing a few facts about **current events or industry trends** makes social conversations **flow effortlessly.**

✓ **Even a little bit of knowledge can make a big difference in how you carry yourself.**

Stay Curious
- **Confidence isn't about knowing everything—it's about being open to learning.**
- A curious mindset **removes the pressure to "have all the answers."**
- Instead of feeling insecure when you don't know something, **see it as an opportunity to learn.**

  Example:
- If a topic comes up that you don't know much about, **instead of shrinking back, ask questions.**
- Saying, *"That's interesting—I'd love to hear more about it,"* makes you **look engaged and intelligent.**

✓ **Confident people don't pretend to know it all—they embrace learning.**

Keep a Growth Mindset

- No one knows it all, but **being willing to learn puts you ahead.**
- A **growth mindset** means you see mistakes and gaps in knowledge as **opportunities to improve, not failures.**

  Example:

- Instead of thinking, *"I'm bad at public speaking,"* shift to *"I can get better with practice."*
- Instead of *"I don't understand this,"* say *"I don't understand this yet."*

√ **Every expert was once a beginner—what matters is the willingness to keep learning.**

Reflection:

Think of a time when:

- You felt confident in a conversation because you were well-informed.
- You learned something new and realized how empowering knowledge can be.
- You stayed curious instead of feeling insecure when you didn't know something.

Knowledge makes you feel ready for anything. The more you learn, the more confident you become—not just in what you know, but in your ability to figure things out.

6. Practice Self-Care

✓ Confidence comes from within—and taking care of yourself is the foundation.

✓ When you prioritize your well-being, you show yourself that you're worth the effort.

You can't feel your best if you're running on empty.

- Self-care isn't just about feeling good in the moment—it's about building **long-term self-respect and confidence.**

- When you **nurture yourself**, you reinforce the message that **you deserve to be cared for, by yourself and others.**

Simple Self-Care Practices:

a. Prioritize Rest and Relaxation

- Sleep **directly affects mood, mental clarity, and confidence.**

- Taking breaks **prevents burnout and keeps your energy high.**

Example:

- Compare how you feel **after a solid 8 hours of sleep** vs. when you're exhausted—your ability to **carry yourself confidently** is completely different.

✓ Rest isn't a luxury—it's a necessity.

b. Fuel Your Body with Nourishing Foods

- **What you eat affects how you feel.**

- A balanced diet helps with **mental clarity, focus, and overall energy levels.**

- Eating well **isn't about restriction—it's about giving your body what it needs to function at its best.**

Example:

- If you've ever felt sluggish after eating junk food vs. energized after a nourishing meal, you know **food influences confidence more than you think.**

✓ **When you fuel your body well, you naturally feel stronger and more capable.**

c. Move Your Body—Walk, Stretch, Dance, Whatever Feels Good

- Physical movement **boosts confidence by improving energy, posture, and overall well-being.**
- Exercise releases **endorphins, which naturally improve mood and self-esteem.**

Example:

- Ever noticed how after a workout or even a short walk, **you feel more clear-headed and in control?**
- Standing up tall, stretching, or dancing around your room **immediately shifts your mood and confidence levels.**

✓ **Your body is meant to move—honoring that helps you feel more connected to yourself.**

d. Take Time for Hobbies or Activities That Bring You Joy

- Doing things you love **reinforces self-worth and confidence.**
- Hobbies remind you that you're **more than your responsibilities—you're a person with passions and interests.**

Example:

- Whether it's **painting, reading, playing an instrument, or cooking—engaging in things you enjoy makes you feel more fulfilled.**

✓ **A confident person is someone who prioritizes their own happiness.**

Why It Works:

When you take care of yourself, you naturally feel more confident.

Self-care isn't selfish—it's proof that you value yourself. The better you feel, the more effortlessly confidence follows.

7. Celebrate Your Wins

✓ **One of the biggest mistakes people make is downplaying their successes.**

✓ **Confidence isn't just about pushing forward—it's about recognizing how far you've already come.**

Every small victory adds up—celebrate yourself.

How to Celebrate Yourself:
Keep a Journal of Daily Wins

- Write down **at least one thing** you accomplished each day—big or small.
- Seeing your progress in writing **reinforces self-confidence and growth.**

Example:

- *"I spoke up in a meeting today."*
- *"I completed a project ahead of schedule."*
- *"I had a difficult conversation and handled it well."*

233

✓ Documenting wins remind you that you are constantly improving.

Treat Yourself When You Achieve a Goal
- **Reward yourself** when you reach a milestone—it reinforces motivation and self-worth.
- The reward doesn't have to be extravagant—it just needs to feel good.

 Example:
- Finished a big project? **Enjoy a nice meal or take the evening off.**
- Completed a personal goal? **Buy yourself something small as a reminder of your progress.**

✓ **Celebrating yourself makes hard work feel worth it.**

Share Your Success With Someone Who Supports You
- **Surround yourself with people who celebrate your growth.**
- Telling a trusted friend or mentor about your win **solidifies it in your mind.**

 Example:
- Text a friend: *"I finally asked for that raise today!"*
- Call someone who always hypes you up and say: *"Guess what? I crushed my presentation!"*

✓ **The more you acknowledge your wins, the more confident you become.**

 Example: A Win is a Win

Did you speak up in a meeting, complete a task, or try something new? That's a win. Own it. Confidence grows when you recognize and affirm your progress.

You don't have to wait for a massive achievement to celebrate yourself—every step forward is proof that you're capable, and that's worth acknowledging.

Your Challenge:

Identify one area where you want to feel more confident. What's one step you can take today to work on it?

Example:

- Want to be more confident speaking in meetings? Commit to sharing one small thought next time.
- Want to improve social confidence? Start a conversation with someone new.
- Want to feel more confident in your skills? Learn something new or practice what you already know.

You are already capable. Now it's time to own it. Step into your confidence—because the world needs the best version of you.

Chapter 18: Understanding Your Skills – Owning Your Gifts & Using Them With Purpose

Your skills come naturally to you. That's why you might not even recognize them as something special. You might assume that because something is easy for you, it must be easy for everyone—but that's not true.

Your skills are unique. Your abilities hold value. Your natural gifts can change lives.

But here's the problem: Many people **downplay their skills** without realizing it. Sometimes, it's because they're humble. Other times, it's because their environment never reflected their greatness back to them. When the people around you don't acknowledge your strengths—**not out of malice, but simply because they don't fully understand them**—you might start to believe they're not that special.

But let me tell you this: **Your skills are needed.** The world is full of problems waiting for solutions. Your strengths, when properly understood and applied, can create solutions, open doors, and shape your entire future. The key is recognizing them, embracing them, and using them with intention.

1. Why Do We Downplay Our Skills?

Here's why so many people overlook their own abilities:

- **It's easy for me, so it must be easy for everyone.** – You don't struggle with it, so you assume it's "average."

- **No one around me talks about my skills.** – Your environment may not recognize or affirm your talents.
- **I've never been rewarded for it.** – No one has paid you or praised you for it, so you assume it's not valuable.
- **I compare myself to "experts."** – You assume your skills don't count unless you're the best in the world at them.
- **I don't see how my skills fit into the bigger picture.** – You don't realize how they can be used in a career, a business, or to help others.

Reality check: Just because something comes naturally to you does **not** mean it's not valuable. Some people struggle to do what you do effortlessly. **Your skills are real, even if you haven't fully recognized them yet.**

2. Your Environment & Your Growth

Not all environments nurture growth. In fact, many environments unintentionally **limit** it. The people around you may love you, but they might not see your potential the way an outside perspective would.

Examples of How Environments Can Limit You:
- Your friends and family don't understand your passion, so they never encourage it.
- You've never seen anyone succeed in what you love doing, so you assume it's not possible.
- Your culture or community values only certain skills (like academic success or traditional careers), so anything outside of that feels "unrealistic."

If your environment has never shown you what's **possible**, it's easy to assume your skills don't matter. **But that's not the truth.**

Solution: Travel. Explore. See Yourself in a New Light. One of the biggest reasons **self-growth tips encourage traveling** is because it shifts your **perspective.** It takes you out of the bubble you've been living in and allows you to see:

✓ How other people value different skills.

✓ How people in different places solve problems in unique ways.

✓ How your skills can serve a real purpose in different industries, cultures, or communities.

Example: Maybe you've always been great at organizing information, but no one in your circle ever needed that skill. Then, while traveling or exploring a new career path, you realize that businesses and entrepreneurs **pay people big money** to structure and organize systems.

Example: Maybe you love writing but never considered it a real skill. Then, you enter a space where storytelling and content creation are highly valued, and suddenly, you see how your words can make an impact.

Lesson? The world needs what you have—it's just a matter of placing yourself in the right spaces to see it.

3. The 3-Part Formula to Find Your Direction

If you're unsure where to take your skills, start with this simple yet powerful formula:

a. Understand Your Strengths

What comes naturally to you? Think about the tasks or skills that feel effortless. What do people compliment you on? What do friends, family, or colleagues often ask you for help with? These are clues to your natural abilities. Your strengths aren't just about what you're good at—they're the things that set you apart, the skills you can refine and leverage to create value in the world.

b. Understand the Problems Around You

Look at the world through a problem-solving lens. What challenges do people face that frustrate them? What gaps exist in industries or communities you're drawn to? Often, the most fulfilling career paths and business ideas stem from solving real problems. The key is to find issues that align with your strengths and passion—when you provide solutions, you create impact.

c. Understand What You Enjoy

What excites you? What activities make you lose track of time? If money wasn't a factor, what work would you still love doing? Passion fuels persistence. When you genuinely enjoy something, you're more likely to stick with it, even when challenges arise. Aligning your work with what excites you makes success feel less like an uphill battle and more like a natural flow.

The Formula in Action:

Your **strengths** + solving a **problem** + what you **love** = a career path, a business idea, or a way to contribute meaningfully to the world.

Example 1:

- **Strength** – You're great at breaking down complex information.
- **Problem** – People struggle with learning certain subjects.
- **Enjoyment** – You love teaching and helping others understand things.
- **Direction?** You might thrive as a content creator, educator, consultant, or coach. You could teach online courses, start a YouTube channel, or create digital guides that simplify learning.

Example 2:
- **Strength** – You have an eye for styling clothes and putting together outfits.
- **Problem** – Many people lack confidence in their wardrobe or don't know how to dress for their body type.
- **Enjoyment** – You love fashion and self-expression.
- **Direction?** You could explore personal styling, fashion blogging, image consulting, or even launching your own clothing brand.

The Power of Alignment

When you align what you're naturally good at with a real-world need and something you genuinely love, you find purpose. This formula not only helps you discover career paths but also helps you refine your niche if you already have a general idea of what you want to do.

The key is not to force yourself into a mold, but to recognize where your unique abilities can make the biggest impact. The best opportunities often come when you step into your natural zone of genius—where skill, purpose, and passion intersect.

Action Step: Take a moment to reflect on your strengths, the problems that intrigue you, and the work that excites you. What connections do you see? What direction is calling you?

4. How to Start Owning Your Skills Today

Too often, we downplay our own abilities, assuming that because something comes easily to us, it must not be special. But the truth is, the skills you take for granted might be the exact thing someone else struggles with. It's time to stop second-guessing yourself and start recognizing your value. Here's how:

a. List 5 Things You're Naturally Good At

Even if they seem small, write them down. Your strengths don't have to be flashy or extraordinary—sometimes, the skills that feel "obvious" to you are the ones that make the biggest impact. Are you great at organizing? Do you give solid advice? Can you explain things in a way that people understand easily? Identifying these strengths is the first step to owning them.

b. Ask 3 People Who Know You Well About Your Strengths

Sometimes, we're too close to our own abilities to see them clearly. Ask three friends, colleagues, or family members what they think your strengths are. You might be surprised at how others perceive you. Often, the things you do naturally—without even thinking—are the ones others admire most.

c. Look at Your Past Wins

Think back to moments where you accomplished something, even if you didn't make a big deal about it at the time. What are achievements you brushed off as "just doing my job" or "no big deal"? Maybe you solved a problem, helped someone, or completed something difficult. Recognizing your past successes reminds you that you are already capable.

d. Stop Comparing Yourself to "Experts"

No one starts as an expert. Every skilled person you admire was once a beginner who dared to start. The key isn't perfection—it's consistent growth. You don't need a certification, a fancy title, or years of experience to be valuable. If you can help someone with your skills today, you already have something worth sharing.

e. Say This Affirmation Daily:

"My skills and abilities are valuable, and I choose to use them with confidence."

Words shape your mindset. Repeating affirmations like this reinforces self-belief and trains your brain to recognize your own value. The more you affirm your skills, the easier it becomes to step into them fully.

The Bottom Line

Your skills deserve to be recognized—first by *you*, then by the world. The sooner you stop downplaying them, the sooner you can start using them to create opportunities, solve problems, and build the life you want. Start today.

5. Final Reminder: Your Skills Are Your Superpower

At the end of the day, **your skills are yours for a reason.** They are part of what makes you unique. The more you recognize them, develop them, and put them to use, the more doors will open for you.

You are not average. You are skilled.

You are not lacking. You are powerful.

You are not invisible. The right people will recognize your value when you recognize it first.

You are sitting on untapped potential. Own it. Use it. The world is waiting for what only you can do.

Chapter 19: Embrace Your Originality

In a world that constantly encourages **comparison, competition, and conformity**, it's easy to measure yourself against others.

We see people who seem **more successful, more talented, more confident, or further along in life**—and suddenly, we start questioning ourselves:

✓ *"Am I good enough?"*

✓ *"Why am I not where they are?"*

✓ *"What if I'll never be as successful as them?"*

But **here's the truth**:

Comparing yourself to someone else is like comparing a bird to a fish—they're made for completely different environments, with their own unique strengths and abilities.

You weren't meant to be a copy of someone else—you were meant to be fully, unapologetically YOU.

This chapter is about **breaking free from comparison and fully embracing your originality.**

1. The Flea in the Jar: Breaking Your Limits

There's an experiment where a **flea—known for its incredible jumping ability—is placed in a jar with a lid.**

At first, the flea **jumps as high as it can, repeatedly hitting the lid.** But over time, it learns to **jump just below the lid** to avoid hitting it.

Eventually, the lid is removed—**but the flea continues jumping at the same limited height, never escaping the jar.**

✓ The flea has **internalized its limitation.**

✓ Even though **nothing is stopping it anymore**, it believes it **can't jump higher.**

The Lesson:

Many of us **are like that flea.**

We've been told:

✓ *"You're not good enough."*

✓ *"You're not smart enough."*

✓ *"You'll never be successful."*

And over time, **we start to believe these limitations**, even when there's **nothing actually stopping us from reaching higher.**

The jar and the lid were never the real problem—the flea's mindset became the real barrier.

Ask Yourself:

- What "lids" have you placed on yourself?
- Are those limits real, or are they assumptions based on fear, past experiences, or comparison?

Example:

- Did someone tell you **you weren't talented enough** to pursue your dream?
- Have past failures made you believe **you'll never succeed?**
- Do you hold back in certain areas of life **because you think you'll fail before you even try?**

The Truth:

You are capable of so much more than you realize.

The only thing keeping you in the jar is **the belief that you can't go further.**

It's time to break free from the jar. Remove the imaginary limits and start reaching for your full potential.

2. Don't Measure Your Abilities by Others'

It's tempting to **look at someone who seems more talented, successful, or confident** and feel **less than.**

But **the truth is—no one's journey is the same.**

You are not here to be a copy of someone else—you are here to become the best version of YOU.

Why Comparison is a Trap:

It's Incomplete – You're comparing your **behind-the-scenes struggles** to someone else's **highlight reel.**

Example:

- You see someone posting their success on social media, but **you don't see the sacrifices, failures, and self-doubt they went through behind closed doors.**
- What looks like **overnight success** is often **years of unseen effort.**

It's Distracting – Focusing on others takes attention **away from your own growth.**

Example:

- If you're constantly watching what everyone else is doing, **when are you working on your own goals?**
- Imagine trying to run a race while staring at someone else's lane—you'll **trip over your own feet instead of focusing forward.**

It's Limiting – Measuring yourself by someone else's abilities **keeps you from reaching your own true potential.** Example:

- A flower doesn't **compare itself to another flower—it just blooms in its own time.**
- What if **your unique strengths** are leading you somewhere completely different than the person you're comparing yourself to?

Focus on This Instead:

✓ **What are your unique strengths and talents?**

✓ **How have you grown or improved over time?**

✓ **What makes you stand out?**

   Example:

- Maybe you're not the loudest person in the room, but **you have deep insight and wisdom.**
- Maybe you're not traditionally "successful" yet, but **your journey is preparing you for something bigger.**
- Maybe you don't fit into the mold of what's "expected," but **that's what makes you irreplaceable.**

Your Path is Yours Alone—Walk It Boldly.

- Stop looking at the **timelines and successes of others** and start focusing on **becoming the best version of YOU.**
- **Your journey isn't meant to look like anyone else's—it's meant to be uniquely yours.**

Your only competition is who you were yesterday. Focus on your growth, your strengths, and your path. Keep moving forward—your success will come in its own time.

3. Everyone Has Their Pros and Cons

No one is perfect—everyone has strengths and weaknesses.

The sooner you accept this about **yourself (and others)**, the more space you create for:

✓ **Growth** – You allow yourself to improve without self-judgment.

✓ **Empathy** – You stop expecting perfection from yourself and others.

✓ **Authenticity** – You embrace who you truly are instead of trying to be someone you're not.

Perfection isn't the goal—self-acceptance is.

The Balance of Strengths and Weaknesses:

Your Pros:

✓ These are the **skills, traits, and abilities** that come naturally to you.

✓ They're what **set you apart and give you an edge.**

Example:

- You might be **great at problem-solving, organizing, or connecting with people.**
- You might have a **knack for creativity, deep thinking, or leadership.**

✓ **Recognizing your strengths allows you to use them to your advantage.**

Your Cons:

✓ These are areas where **you struggle—but they don't define you.**

✓ Everyone has weaknesses—but **they don't take away from your value.**

Example:

- Maybe you **struggle with public speaking, staying focused, or time management.**
- Maybe you **tend to overthink, procrastinate, or get nervous in new situations.**

✓ Your weaknesses don't make you "less than"—they just highlight areas for growth.

The Key:

✓ **Don't let your weaknesses overshadow your strengths.**

✓ **Instead of dwelling on what you lack, recognize what makes you uniquely capable.**

✓ **Work on improving your weaknesses, but don't let them define your self-worth.**

Example:

- If you're not great at public speaking, focus on **writing your thoughts clearly** instead.
- If you struggle with time management, **create routines that keep you on track.**
- If you're not naturally outgoing, **lean into your ability to connect in deeper, meaningful ways.**

✓ **Your weaknesses don't make you inadequate—they make you human.**

4. The Danger of Comparison: A Real-Life Example

Imagine **two artists.**

One paints realistic portraits.

The other creates abstract designs.

If the abstract artist **compares themselves to the portrait artist,** they might feel **inferior—thinking, "I'm not as skilled as them."**

But the beauty of art is its **diversity—no style is inherently "better" than the other.**

Each artist has a unique strength that makes their work special. A realistic painter captures fine details, while an abstract artist conveys emotion in a way realism never could.

The world needs both.

The Takeaway:

You're not meant to excel in the same way as someone else. Your originality is what makes you valuable.

Example:

- If you compare yourself to someone excelling in their lane, **you might overlook your own strengths.**
- A singer with a deep, soulful voice shouldn't feel less talented because they don't sound like a pop star.
- A writer who thrives in storytelling shouldn't feel inadequate just because they don't write technical articles.

✓ **You were designed to be YOU—not a lesser version of someone else.**

Own Your Style. Own Your Gifts. Own What Makes You Different.

- Stop **measuring yourself by someone else's abilities** and start **embracing your own.**
- **Comparison blinds you to your own uniqueness.**
- **What sets you apart is what makes you irreplaceable.**

There's only one you—lean into that fully.

5. Everyone is Original

No two people have the same:

- **Experiences** – Everything you've been through shapes how you see the world.
- **Perspectives** – The way you interpret things is completely unique to you.
- **Talents** – No one has the exact same blend of skills, strengths, and creativity as you do.

Even if **two people share similar interests, backgrounds, or goals**, their approach will **always be different**—because **they are different.**

Why Originality Matters:

Your Perspective is Unique – No one else sees or experiences life exactly like you.

Example:

- Two people can **look at the same painting** and take away **two completely different emotions or meanings.**
- Your perspective **brings value because it's yours alone.**

Your Journey is Your Own – Your **story, struggles, and lessons** all have value.

Example:

- No one else has walked the exact path you have.

- Your unique combination of **challenges, victories, and growth** has given you wisdom that **no one else can replicate.**

Your Impact is Different – The way you **influence others, solve problems, or create** is entirely yours.

Example:

- Maybe you inspire others by **the way you listen, lead, or support.**
- Maybe you have a skill that **helps others in a way no one else does.**
- The **ripple effect of your actions** can change lives in ways you might not even realize.

Reflection:

✓ **Think of one thing that makes you uniquely you—something no one else can replicate.**

✓ **That's your originality, and it's worth celebrating.**

Example:

- Maybe you have a way of **turning serious moments into laughter.**
- Maybe you **see patterns or solutions that others miss.**
- Maybe your **compassion, creativity, or resilience** sets you apart.

Your originality isn't just **something nice to have—it's your power. Own it. Embrace it. Share it with the world.**

6. Let Go of the Need to Compare

Comparison is the fastest way to drain your confidence and joy.

It shifts your focus from **your strengths** to **what you think you're missing.**

Here's how to stop comparing yourself to others and start embracing your own journey:

Focus on Your Growth

✓ Instead of looking at others, **track your own progress and wins.**

✓ Measure yourself **against who you were yesterday—not against someone else's timeline.**

   Example:
   - If you've improved in any area of your life, **that's progress worth celebrating.**
   - Maybe you're learning a skill, becoming more patient, or handling challenges better.

   Your path is YOURS. Keep building on it.

Celebrate Others Without Diminishing Yourself

✓ Someone else's success **doesn't take away from your own potential.**

✓ Instead of feeling intimidated, **let it inspire you.**

   Example:
   - If someone gets a promotion, instead of thinking *"I'll never get there,"* shift to *"If they can do it, so can I."*
   - If you see someone excelling, **study their process instead of envying their results.**

   Success isn't a competition—there's room for everyone to grow.

Practice Gratitude

✓ Shift your focus from **what you lack to what you have.**

✓ Gratitude rewires your brain to see abundance instead of scarcity.

    Example:

- Instead of thinking *"I wish I had their life,"* remind yourself of what's going well in yours.

- You might already have things someone else wishes they had. **Focusing on your blessings makes comparison lose its power.**

Limit Exposure to Triggers

✓ If social media, certain environments, or conversations **make you feel less than, take a step back.**

✓ Be intentional about **what you consume and who you surround yourself with.**

    Example:

- If scrolling Instagram makes you feel behind, **take a break from it.**

- If certain people constantly make you feel inadequate, **set boundaries.**

Protect your peace by choosing where you place your energy. The Only Person You Need to Be Better Than Is the Person You Were Yesterday.

Reflection Exercise: Embracing Your Originality

1. Write down three things that make you uniquely you.

✓ What skills, traits, or perspectives do you have that no one else can replicate?

✔ Maybe it's your creativity, your sense of humor, your ability to make people feel comfortable—whatever it is, own it.

2. Think about a time when you compared yourself to someone else.

✔ What did you learn from that experience?

✔ Did comparison make you feel motivated, or did it drain your confidence?

✔ How can you shift your mindset from **comparison to self-appreciation?**

3. Identify one "lid" you've placed on yourself—and take a step to remove it.

✔ What limitation have you believed about yourself that might not even be true?

✔ What's one action you can take today to **challenge that limit and prove to yourself that you're capable of more?**

Final Thoughts

You are **not** a flea in a jar.

✔ You are **limitless.**

✔ You are **original.**

✔ You are **full of untapped potential.**

While it's important to learn from others and do the inner work, remember:

You are not defined by others' abilities or achievements. Your worth isn't measured by comparison—it's measured by your own growth.

Your journey is unique, and your originality is your greatest asset.

No one else has your exact perspective, skills, or experiences—that is your superpower.

Focus on being better than you were yesterday—not better than someone else.

You're not in competition with anyone. Your only goal is to keep evolving into your best self.

The World Needs YOU—Exactly as You Are.

Step into your power.

Trust in your journey.

And most of all—be unapologetically YOU.

Chapter 20: The Role of Gratitude in Living With Purpose

Gratitude is one of the **simplest yet most powerful** tools for living with **intention and purpose.**

It's easy to get caught up in:

✓ **What's missing.**

✓ **What's next.**

✓ **What could be better.**

But **gratitude shifts your focus** from **lack to abundance,** helping you recognize **the beauty in everyday moments.**

When practiced consistently, gratitude can:

- **Rewire your brain** to focus on the positive. **Example:** The more you practice gratitude, the more your brain **naturally** looks for things to appreciate.

- **Improve your relationships** by deepening appreciation for others.
  Example: When you express gratitude for someone, it strengthens your bond and helps them feel valued.

- **Ground you in the present,** creating a deeper sense of contentment.
  Example: Instead of **chasing happiness in the future,** gratitude helps you find joy **right now, in this moment.**

Gratitude Doesn't Just Happen When Life is Good

✓ It's easy to be grateful **when everything is going well.**

✓ But true gratitude **is a mindset—it allows you to find good, even in the difficult moments.**

Example:

- Maybe you're facing a challenge, but **there's still something to be thankful for—a lesson, a moment of support, or the strength to keep going.**
- Gratitude helps you **shift your perspective** so that even setbacks become part of your growth.

1. What is Gratitude?

Gratitude is **more than just saying "thank you"**—it's an **intentional way of thinking** that shifts your focus to **appreciation,** no matter what's happening in your life.

It's about **choosing to see what's present, rather than what's missing.**

Why Gratitude is Powerful:
It helps you see abundance instead of scarcity.

Example: Instead of thinking, *"I don't have enough,"* gratitude shifts your mindset to *"I have so much to be thankful for."*

It cultivates positivity and resilience.

Example: When life gets tough, gratitude reminds you that even in challenges, **there's something good to hold onto.**

It strengthens connections with others by recognizing their impact.

Example: When you appreciate people—whether it's a friend, family member, or coworker—it deepens relationships and brings more kindness into your life.

Gratitude isn't just a reaction to good things—it's a practice of seeking good, even in difficult situations.

✓ You don't need **everything to be perfect** to be grateful.

✓ You can **find something to appreciate, even on the hardest days.**

✓ The more you practice gratitude, **the more you naturally start seeing the good in everything.**

Reflection Question:
When was the last time you felt truly grateful for something? Take a moment to reflect—**what was it, and how did it make you feel?**

2. The Science Behind Gratitude

Gratitude isn't just a **"feel-good" concept**—scientific studies have proven its **measurable benefits** for both **mental and physical health.**

When practiced consistently, gratitude **rewires your brain** to focus on **positivity, resilience, and well-being.**

The Proven Benefits of Gratitude:
1. Improved Mood
Gratitude boosts **dopamine and serotonin,** two neurotransmitters responsible for **happiness and emotional well-being.**

People who practice gratitude consistently have **lower levels of anxiety and depression.**

Example:

- Keeping a **daily gratitude journal** has been shown to **increase overall happiness and reduce stress.**
- Even on difficult days, finding **one thing to be grateful for** can shift your emotional state.

2. Stronger Relationships

Expressing gratitude **deepens trust, appreciation, and emotional intimacy.**

Grateful people make others feel **valued, respected, and seen,** which strengthens bonds in **friendships, family, and romantic relationships.**

Example:

- A simple **"I appreciate you"** can strengthen a relationship **far more than people realize.**
- Couples who express **gratitude regularly** tend to have **stronger, more connected relationships.**

3. Increased Resilience

When you focus on gratitude, you **train your brain** to find **strength in challenges** instead of only seeing struggles. Gratitude shifts your perspective—**instead of asking, "Why is this happening to me?" you ask, "What can I learn from this?"**

Example:

- Many successful people attribute their ability to **overcome setbacks** to gratitude—because it allows them to see difficulties as **stepping stones rather than roadblocks.**
- When facing a challenge, **writing down three things you're grateful for** can help you approach it with **a clearer, stronger mindset.**

4. Enhanced Sleep

Studies show that **reflecting on what you're grateful for before bed** leads to **better, deeper sleep.**

Gratitude helps **reduce racing thoughts, stress, and negative thinking** that often keep people awake.

Example:
- Instead of replaying worries from the day, **write down three positive moments before bed.**
- This trains your brain to **end the day on a peaceful note, leading to improved rest.**

Reflection Question:

How would your life change if you focused more on what you're grateful for instead of what's missing?

Take a moment to reflect—**how could shifting your mindset to gratitude improve your mood, relationships, or ability to handle challenges?**

3. Gratitude in Action: How to Practice It

Building a gratitude practice doesn't have to be complicated. Here are some **simple, powerful** ways to **infuse gratitude** into your daily life:

a. Keep a Gratitude Journal

Each day, **write down 3-5 things you're grateful for.** These can be **big or small**—a supportive friend, a hot cup of coffee, or simply the fact that you made it through the day. Reflect on **why these things matter** and how they make you feel.

Example:

Instead of writing, *"I'm grateful for my best friend."*

Write: *"I'm grateful for my best friend because she always listens without judgment and makes me feel understood."*

Why It Works:

✓ Writing things down **trains your brain** to notice and appreciate the **positives in everyday life.**

✓ Over time, this **rewires your thinking** to focus on **abundance instead of lack.**

b. Express Gratitude to Others

Tell people when you **appreciate them.**

Send a **text, write a note, or say it in person.**

Be specific: Instead of saying *"Thanks for everything,"* say, *"Thank you for listening to me today—it really helped me feel supported."*

Why It Works:

✓ **Gratitude makes others feel seen, valued, and appreciated.**

✓Strengthens relationships by reinforcing the **positive moments** you share with others.

✓ It **creates a cycle of kindness**—when people feel appreciated, they're more likely to pass that energy forward.

c. Practice Mindful Gratitude Throughout Your Day

Take **mini-moments** to pause and appreciate **the little things.** Notice and **feel grateful for:**

- The **smell of your coffee** in the morning.
- A **beautiful sunset** that makes you pause.
- A **stranger's kind gesture**—a smile, a door held open, a compliment.

Why It Works:

- When you **train your brain to appreciate small joys,** they start adding up—making your **daily life feel richer and more fulfilling.**
- It **reduces stress** by shifting your focus to **what's going right.**

Example:

You might have a **stressful day at work,** but if you take a moment to **appreciate the small joys**, you'll end the day with **a more balanced perspective.**

d. Turn Challenges into Gratitude

When facing difficulties, **ask yourself:**

✓ *"What is this teaching me?"*

✓ *"How can I grow from this?"*

Why It Works:

✓ Finding **gratitude in hardships** doesn't mean **ignoring pain**—it's about recognizing the **strength, lessons, or new opportunities they bring.**

Example:

- **A breakup** might be painful, but it can also teach you **self-worth and personal growth.**
- **Losing a job** may feel discouraging, but it can **open doors to better opportunities.**
- **A difficult conversation** might feel uncomfortable, but it can **lead to deeper understanding and stronger relationships.**

Reflection Question:

Can you think of a difficult experience that ultimately led to something positive?

How did it shape your **growth, mindset, or perspective?**

4. The Ripple Effect of Gratitude

Gratitude **doesn't just change how you feel**—it changes how you **interact with the world** and **how others respond to you.**

When you practice gratitude, you **inspire those around you** to do the same, creating a **positive chain reaction.**

Examples of the Ripple Effect:

In Relationships:

Expressing gratitude **deepens trust and connection.** When people **feel appreciated,** they're more likely to **return kindness and generosity.**

Example:

- A simple **"I really appreciate you"** to a partner or friend can **strengthen your bond** and make them feel valued.
- When you express **gratitude regularly,** people are **more likely to feel safe, heard, and respected in your presence.**

At Work:

Gratitude **creates a positive atmosphere,** increasing **motivation and teamwork.**

A simple **"thank you"** to a colleague can **boost morale and strengthen collaboration.**

Example:

- A manager who **regularly acknowledges their team's efforts** will have **more engaged, motivated employees.**
- Even a coworker saying, **"I really admire how you handled that situation,"** can make someone's day.

Why It Works:

- People work **harder and feel more committed** when they feel appreciated.
- Gratitude **reduces workplace stress** and fosters **team unity.**

In Your Community:

Acts of gratitude—like **volunteering, helping a neighbor, or simply being kind**—create a **ripple of kindness and connection.** A single act of appreciation can **inspire others to pass it forward.**

Example:

- Holding the door open for someone or **thanking a cashier for their service** can brighten their day.
- Small, genuine moments of gratitude can **make a stranger feel seen and valued.**

Why It Works:
- People who **experience kindness and appreciation** are more likely to **spread that energy** to others.
- Gratitude fosters **stronger, more connected communities.**

5. Gratitude and Living With Purpose

When you practice gratitude, you naturally start living with more intention.

✓ Gratitude shifts your mindset from **chasing more** to **appreciating what's already here.**

✓ It reminds you that **life isn't just about the end goal—it's about appreciating the journey.**

How Gratitude Grounds You in Purpose:
It Keeps You Present:

✓ Instead of constantly **thinking about what's next,** gratitude reminds you to enjoy **where you are.**

✓ The little moments—**conversations, experiences, and acts of kindness—are what truly make life meaningful.**

Example:
- A person striving for career success might focus so much on their **next promotion** that they forget to appreciate how far they've already come.

- Practicing gratitude helps them **recognize their progress, the people who supported them, and the experiences that shaped them.**

It Helps You Appreciate Challenges:

✓ Gratitude isn't just about being thankful for **good things**—it's about **finding value in the hard times too.**

✓ Challenges often lead to **growth, resilience, and lessons that shape us.**

Example:

- A difficult breakup might teach someone **self-worth and independence.**
- A career setback might open the door to **a better opportunity.**
- A health struggle might lead to **a deeper appreciation for well-being.**

Reframing struggles through gratitude helps you recognize that even difficulties serve a purpose.

It Aligns You With What Truly Matters:

✓ When you focus on **what you're grateful for,** you naturally align yourself with **your values and priorities.**

✓ Gratitude helps filter out **distractions, unnecessary worries, and societal pressures.**

Example:

- Instead of comparing yourself to others, gratitude reminds you of **your own unique path.**

- Instead of focusing on what you lack, gratitude highlights **what's already abundant in your life.**

Questions to Reflect On:
- What am I most grateful for right now?
- How can I show gratitude for both the opportunities and challenges in my life?
- Who or what has had the biggest impact on my journey— and how can I honor that?

Gratitude doesn't just make life feel better—it connects you to your purpose, your values, and what truly matters.

Reflection Exercise: Cultivating Gratitude

Gratitude isn't just something you feel—it's something you **practice consistently** until it becomes a natural part of your mindset.

Here are **three powerful exercises** to help you cultivate a daily habit of gratitude:

a. Daily Gratitude Practice

Before bed, take a few moments to write down **one moment that brought you joy** or something you appreciated that day.

✓ It can be as simple as:
- "Had a great conversation with a friend."
- "The weather was perfect today."
- "I felt proud of myself for getting through a tough situation."

Why It Works:
- It rewires your brain to **focus on the good, even on tough days.**

- Over time, it trains you to **naturally seek moments of gratitude throughout your day.**

b. The Gratitude Letter

Write a heartfelt letter to someone who has **positively impacted your life.**

You **don't even have to send it**—just writing it down is powerful on its own.

Example Prompts:

✓ "I want to thank you for..."

✓ "You have made a difference in my life by..."

✓ "Something you did that I'll never forget is..."

Why It Works:

✓ Expressing gratitude **deepens your appreciation** for others.

✓ If you choose to send it, it can **strengthen relationships and brighten someone's day.**

c. The Gratitude Jar

Find a jar and keep it somewhere visible.

Every time you experience **a moment of gratitude,** write it on a small piece of paper and place it in the jar.

Over time, this becomes a **visual reminder of all the good in your life.**

Example Entries:

- "Had an amazing meal today."
- "Got a compliment from a coworker."
- "Heard my favorite song at the perfect moment."

Why It Works:

✓ On hard days, you can **pull out a note** and remind yourself of the good that exists in your life.

✓ It helps you recognize **how much you already have to be grateful for.**

Final Thoughts

✓ **Gratitude is the foundation of a purposeful life.**

✓ It doesn't require **money, resources, or perfect circumstances**— it's a **mindset available to everyone.**

✓ The more you **practice gratitude,** the easier it becomes to **live with joy, connection, and fulfillment.**

When you choose to focus on what you have instead of what you lack, your entire world changes. Gratitude is a daily decision, and it's one that can transform your life in ways you never imagined. A simple "thank you," a moment of appreciation, or a shift in perspective can be the spark that brightens your day—or someone else's. Be the reason someone smiles today.

Chapter 21: Overcoming Fear of Failure

Failure. Just the word itself can bring feelings of **doubt, embarrassment, or fear.** But what if failure wasn't something to **avoid**—what if it was something to **embrace?**

✓ Society teaches us that **failure is bad**—that it's a sign of **weakness or incompetence.**

✓ In reality, **failure is an essential part of success.**

✓ Every setback you face holds a **lesson, a redirection, or an opportunity to grow.**

The most successful people in the world failed—many times. The difference? They didn't let failure stop them.

1. Why Are We So Afraid of Failure?

The fear of failure runs deep—it's tied to our need for **acceptance, security, and validation.** We often equate failure with **rejection, embarrassment, or even a personal flaw.**

Common   Thoughts   That   Fuel   Fear   of   Failure:

✓ *"What will people think of me?"*

✓ *"What if I'm not good enough?"*

✓ *"What if I lose everything I've worked for?"*

But here's the truth: **Failure isn't the opposite of success—it's part of the process.**

Reframing Failure:

Instead of asking, *"What if I fail?"*

✓ Start asking, *"What will I learn if I fail?"*

Why This Mindset Shift Matters:

✓ It turns **fear into curiosity.**

✓ It helps you see **challenges as stepping stones instead of roadblocks.**

✓ It reminds you that **failure doesn't define you—your response to it does.**

When you **reframe failure as feedback,** you stop fearing it and start **using it to your advantage.**

2. The Truth About Failure

The most successful people in the world didn't avoid failure—they **embraced it, learned from it, and used it as fuel.**

Here are three powerful examples of people who turned failure into their greatest advantage:

1. Steven Spielberg – Rejected from Film School Three Times

The legendary filmmaker applied to the **University of Southern California's (USC) film school** three times—and was rejected **every single time.**

Instead of giving up, he enrolled at another university and **pursued his passion relentlessly.**

Today, Spielberg is one of the most celebrated directors in history, known for movies like *Jurassic Park, Schindler's List,* and *E.T.*

✓ **Lesson:** *Sometimes rejection is redirection.* A "no" today doesn't mean "no" forever.

2. Vera Wang – Failed Figure Skater Turned Fashion Icon

Before becoming one of the **most successful fashion designers** in the world, Vera Wang had dreams of becoming an Olympic figure skater.

She trained for years, but after **failing to qualify** for the **1968 U.S. Olympic team,** her dreams were crushed.

Instead of dwelling on disappointment, she **pivoted to fashion**—and today, she is a **household name** in bridal wear and luxury design.

Lesson: *Failure forces you to pivot, but sometimes that pivot leads you to something even greater.*

3. Walt Disney – Fired for "Lacking Creativity"

Before building the **Disney empire,** Walt Disney worked at a newspaper—until his editor **fired him for "lacking imagination."**

Then, he started an animation company that **went bankrupt.**

But through years of **trial, error, and setbacks,** he refused to give up—eventually creating one of the most **beloved and influential** entertainment companies of all time.

Lesson: *Failure doesn't mean you lack talent. It simply means your success is still in the making.*

What These Stories Teach Us:

✓ **Rejection isn't the end—it's just part of the journey.**

✓ **Failure doesn't define you—your resilience does.**

✓ **Sometimes setbacks push you toward something even greater.**

The key is to keep going.

3. Reframing Failure

The way you **view** failure determines how it **impacts** you.

If you see failure as a **final defeat**, it will stop you.

✔ But if you see it as **feedback**, it will fuel you.

Shift Your Perspective on Failure:

From Defeat to Feedback:

Failure isn't a verdict—it's information. Instead of seeing it as the end, ask yourself:

✔ *"What went wrong?"*

✔ *"What can I do differently next time?"*

From Fear to Curiosity:

Instead of dreading failure, **approach it with curiosity.**

✔ *"What will this experience teach me?"*

✔ *"How can this setback make me stronger?"*

From a Fixed to a Growth Mindset:

A fixed mindset sees failure as **proof of inadequacy**—"I'm just not good at this."

✔ **A growth mindset** sees failure as an **opportunity to improve**—"I can learn and get better at this."

Example of This Mindset Shift in Action:

Instead of thinking, *"I failed at this job interview, so I must not be good enough,"*

Try, *"That interview taught me where I need to improve. Next time, I'll be better prepared."*

Reflection Question:
Can you recall a time when failure led to an unexpected success?
Sometimes what feels like failure is just a redirection toward something even better.

4. Why Failure is Necessary for Growth

Failure isn't just something to **accept**—it's something to **embrace**.
It pushes you out of your comfort zone and **challenges** you to adapt, innovate, and grow.

What Failure Teaches You:
Resilience:
✓ Every failure you overcome **makes you stronger**.
✓ You learn that setbacks **don't define you**—your ability to rise does.

Creativity:
✓ When Plan A fails, you're forced to **think outside the box**.
✓ Some of the greatest innovations came from **mistakes** (like Post-it Notes and penicillin).

Self-Awareness:
✓ Failure teaches you **what works and what doesn't**.

✓ It highlights **your strengths, weaknesses, and areas for improvement.**

The Bigger Picture:
Failure **isn't a detour**—it's part of the **road to success.**
Example:
Every great athlete, artist, and entrepreneur has failed—**multiple times.**
The difference? They **didn't quit.** They **learned, adjusted,** and **kept going.**
The lesson? Every failure **prepares you for your next success.**

5. How to Overcome the Fear of Failure

Fear of failure can be **paralyzing,** but it **doesn't have to control you.**

Here are **actionable steps** to **shift your mindset** and move past fear:

a. Redefine Failure

Exercise: Write down what failure **means to you**—then rewrite it as a **positive statement.**

Negative Belief: "Failure means I'm not good enough."

✓ **New Perspective:** "Failure means I'm learning and growing."

Why It Works: The way you **define failure** determines how you **react to it.**

b. Take Small Risks

Start with **low-stakes risks** to **build confidence** in facing failure.

✓ Try a **new hobby** you've never done before.

✓ Speak up **in a meeting** or share your thoughts in a conversation.

✓ Share an **idea**, even if it's not fully formed or "perfect."

The more you take small risks, the more you realize failure isn't as scary as it seems.

c. Focus on Effort, Not Outcome

✓ You **can't control** the result, but you **can control** your **effort**.

✓ Celebrate **trying**, even if things don't go as planned.

Example:

Instead of saying, *"I failed at launching my business"*, say: "I took a huge step forward, and I learned valuable lessons for my next attempt."

Why It Works: You build confidence by **valuing progress** over perfection.

d. Learn from Failure

After every setback, ask yourself:

✓ "What **went well?**"

✓ "What **didn't go as planned?**"

✓ "What **can I do differently** next time?"

Example:

- A writer gets rejected by a publisher. Instead of giving up, they **improve their draft** and submit again.

- A person fails a job interview. Instead of feeling defeated, they **refine their answers** and gain confidence for the next one.

Lesson: Failure isn't the **end**—it's a **lesson.**

e. Separate Failure from Identity

Failing at something does not mean you are a failure.

"I failed, so I'm not good at this."

✓ "This didn't work, but that doesn't define me—I can improve."

Why It Works: One failure doesn't **define you**—how you **respond** does.

f. Visualize Success

✓ Instead of obsessing over **what could go wrong**, focus on **what success looks like.**

✓ Imagine yourself **overcoming obstacles** and **achieving your goal.**

Example:

Before a big presentation, visualize yourself **speaking with confidence** and **receiving positive reactions.** Before launching a new project, picture **yourself succeeding**, even if challenges arise.

Reflection Question:

What **fear of failure** is **holding you back** right now? And what **small step** can you take to **move past it**?

278

Every failure is just a stepping stone toward success. Keep going.

6. Failure as Fuel for Success

Failure doesn't just **teach**—it can also **ignite** your drive to keep pushing forward.

Instead of seeing it as a **roadblock**, use failure as **fuel** to become stronger, smarter, and more resilient.

How to Turn Failure into Motivation:
Use Setbacks as Stepping Stones
What to Do:

✓ After a failure, **reframe it** into a stepping stone by setting a new, **adjusted goal**.

✓ Instead of dwelling on what went wrong, **focus on the next move**.

> **Example:**
> - If your business idea didn't take off, analyze why and refine your strategy for the next attempt.
> - If you didn't pass a test, study your weak points and retake it with better preparation.

Channel Frustration into Action
What to Do:

✓ Instead of letting failure bring you down, let it **fuel your determination**.

✓ Tell yourself: *"I won't let this be the end of my story."*

> **Example:**

An athlete who loses a competition trains harder to come back stronger.

A writer who gets rejected by publishers uses it as motivation to write an even better book.

Look at Past Failures You've Overcome

What to Do:

✓ Think about failures you've **already conquered**—those moments when you thought you failed but later realized they were just **stepping stones**.

✓ Use them as **proof** that you can **overcome anything** again.

    Example:

Remember when you struggled with something new (like learning a skill or starting a job) but eventually **got better**?

That's proof that **this setback is just another challenge to overcome**.

Success Isn't About Never Failing—It's About Refusing to Quit.

    Failure **only wins** if you **stop trying**.

✓ Keep learning.

✓ Keep adjusting.

✓ Keep moving forward.

    Your next success is waiting on the other side of persistence.

Reflection Exercise: Embracing Failure

Take a moment to reflect on your relationship with failure and how you can **reframe it** into a tool for growth.

a. Think of a Past Failure:

- **What happened?** Write down a failure you experienced.
- **What did you learn from it?** Reflect on the lessons it taught you.
- **How did it help you grow?** Identify how it shaped you into a stronger, wiser, or more resilient person.

Example:
- Maybe you didn't get a job you wanted, but it led you to a better opportunity.
- Maybe you made a mistake in a relationship, but it taught you how to communicate better.

b. Reframe Your Current Fear:
- What's something you're afraid to try because of fear of failure?
- Write down the worst-case scenario. Is it really as bad as you think?
- Write down the best-case scenario. What could go right if you succeed?

Example:

- **Fear:** Starting a new business.
- **Worst Case:** It doesn't work out, and I have to try something different.
- **Best Case:** It becomes a success, and I create something amazing.

Now ask yourself: Is the fear of failure worth holding me back from my best-case scenario?

c. Set a Growth Goal:

- What is one small step you can take today to face your fear?
- Action makes fear lose its power—commit to one small move forward.

Example:

- If you're afraid of public speaking, practice speaking in front of a mirror.
- If you're afraid of applying for a job, submit one application today.
- If you're afraid of failure in a personal goal, take the first small step toward it.

Growth comes from taking action, even when you're afraid.

Final Thoughts: Redefining Failure

Failure isn't the opposite of success—it's part of the path to success. It's the **teacher** that shapes you, the **lesson** that strengthens you, and the **challenge** that prepares you for your greatest achievements.

Every successful person you admire has faced setbacks—probably more than you can imagine. **The difference?** They kept going. They saw failure as feedback, not defeat. And that's exactly what you should do too.

✓ **Failure is proof that you're trying.**

✓ **Failure builds resilience, strength, and wisdom.**

✓ **Failure isn't the end—unless you stop moving forward.**

Chapter 22: Building a Life of Purpose Through Small Habits

Big dreams often feel overwhelming, as though they are distant mountains too steep to climb. But the secret to achieving them isn't found in giant leaps—it's in the small, consistent actions you take every day. Your habits shape your routine, mindset, and, ultimately, your future. They are the quiet forces that determine whether you move closer to your aspirations or drift further away.

When you intentionally build habits that align with your goals and values, you create a strong foundation for a fulfilling and purpose-driven life. These daily choices, however small, compound over time, leading to lasting transformation. Whether it's improving your health, sharpening your mind, or strengthening relationships, purposeful habits serve as the stepping stones that guide you toward the life you envision.

Cultivating meaningful, intentional habits can create long-term success and happiness. By focusing on small but impactful changes, you can gradually shape a life that reflects your deepest aspirations, one step at a time.

1. The Power of Small Habits

At first glance, habits might seem insignificant—just tiny, routine actions that don't make much of a difference. But over time, these small choices compound into remarkable results, shaping the trajectory of your life in ways you may not even realize. This is known as the **Compound Effect**: small, consistent actions accumulate, leading to exponential growth and transformation.

Think of habits like drops of water filling a jar. Each drop might seem inconsequential on its own, but eventually, the jar overflows. The same principle applies to the choices you make every day—whether positive or negative, they add up and determine the direction of your future.

Real-Life Examples of the Compound Effect in Action

Reading just 10 pages a day might not seem like much, but over the course of a year, that adds up to **3,650 pages**—the equivalent of about **12 books**. That's a dozen opportunities to expand your knowledge, shift your mindset, and gain new perspectives.

Drinking one extra glass of water daily might feel trivial, but over time, it leads to **better hydration, improved skin health, and higher energy levels**—small benefits that contribute to long-term well-being.

Saving just $5 a day may not seem significant, but in a year, that's **$1,825** saved—enough for a vacation, an investment, or a financial safety net.

These small, intentional actions may feel minor in the moment, but their **cumulative effect** can be life-changing.

Why Small Habits Work

They're easier to stick to. Unlike drastic changes that often feel overwhelming, small habits are manageable and don't require a huge amount of effort or motivation.

They build momentum and confidence. When you see progress—even in small ways—you feel more motivated to keep going. Success, no matter how minor, reinforces your belief in your ability to improve.

They create a ripple effect. Good habits don't just stay in one area of your life; they influence other aspects as well. A morning workout might lead to healthier food choices, which in turn improves your energy and focus at work.

At the core of it all, your **habits shape your future**, whether you're conscious of it or not. Every small choice you make today is a step toward the life you are creating. The question is: **Are your current habits leading you toward the life you want?** If not, it's time to take control—one small step at a time.

2. The 21/90 Rule: How Long Does It Take to Form a Habit?

You've probably heard the saying that it takes **21 days to form a habit and 90 days to make it a permanent part of your lifestyle.** But why is this the case? The process of habit formation isn't just about willpower—it's about rewiring your brain through **consistent repetition** until the action becomes second nature.

Breaking Down the 21/90 Rule:

21 Days: This is the adjustment phase. Your brain starts recognizing the new behavior, and while it still takes conscious effort, it begins to feel familiar. At this stage, consistency is key—you're laying the groundwork for a lasting habit.

90 Days: By this point, the habit becomes a **part of your identity**. It's no longer something you have to force yourself to do; it just feels natural. You don't think about brushing your teeth every morning—you just do it. The same principle applies to any new habit when repeated long enough.

Think of habits like **muscle memory**—the more you practice, the easier it becomes. At first, a new routine might feel uncomfortable or unnatural, but with enough repetition, it shifts from being something you *do* to something you *are*.

Example in Action:

Waking up early: At first, dragging yourself out of bed before sunrise might feel like torture. But after **21 days** of setting your alarm and resisting the snooze button, your body starts adjusting. By **90 days**, waking up early no longer feels like a chore—it's just part of your day.

Exercising regularly: The first few weeks of working out can be tough, but after 21 days, your body adapts to the routine. By 90 days, fitness becomes part of your lifestyle, and skipping a workout feels unnatural.

Healthy eating: Cutting out junk food might seem impossible at first, but after three weeks of making mindful choices, it gets easier. By three months, nutritious eating feels automatic rather than restrictive.

The Secret to Success? Consistency.

Building a habit isn't about perfection—it's about persistence. Some days will be harder than others, and that's okay. The key is to **keep going** even when motivation fades.

Commit to 21 days to get started, and push through to 90 days to make it part of your lifestyle. Once you reach that point, the habit is no longer something you have to force—it's simply who you are.

3. Align Your Habits with Your Goals

To build a life of purpose, your **habits must reflect your values and long-term aspirations**. Otherwise, you'll find yourself stuck in routines that don't serve you—busy but not productive, active but not progressing. Every habit you build should act as a stepping stone, bringing you closer to the future you envision.

Ask Yourself:

What's most important to me? (Health, relationships, career, personal growth?)

What are my long-term goals? (Where do I see myself in 1, 5, or 10 years?)

What small, daily actions can move me closer to those goals?

The Key: Micro-Habits That Support Your Bigger Vision

Instead of focusing on drastic, unsustainable changes, create small, intentional habits that align with your goals. These tiny actions **compound over time**, making massive transformation feel effortless.

Examples of Goal-Aligned Habits:

Goal: Improve your health.

Habit: Drink a glass of water first thing in the morning or take a 10-minute walk daily.

Goal: Grow your knowledge.

Habit: Read one chapter of a book every night before bed or listen to an educational podcast on your commute.

Goal: Strengthen relationships.
Habit: Send a thoughtful message to a friend or loved one every day.

Goal: Advance in your career.
Habit: Spend 15 minutes each morning learning a new skill or networking with someone in your field.

Goal: Become more mindful and present.
Habit: Start each day with a 5-minute meditation or gratitude journaling.

Are Your Habits Helping or Hindering You?

Your daily habits should be a reflection of the life you're building. If they aren't, it's time to **make adjustments**. Look at your current routines—are they **guiding you toward** your goals or **keeping you in place**? If something isn't serving you, let it go and replace it with a habit that does.

By **aligning your daily actions with your dreams**, you ensure that every step you take is leading you closer to the **life you truly want**.

4. How to Create Purposeful Habits

Building habits that **stick** isn't just about willpower—it requires strategy and intention. The reason many people struggle with habits is that they try to change too much at once or set goals that are too vague. Instead, you need a **structured approach** that makes new behaviors easy to adopt and maintain. Here's how to create habits that last:

a. Start Small

One of the biggest mistakes people make when forming new habits is trying to do too much at once. Drastic changes can feel overwhelming, making it harder to stay consistent. Instead, **focus on one habit at a time and start small**.

Instead of saying, "I'll work out for an hour every day," **Start with:** "I'll do 5-10 minutes of movement each morning."

Small habits are **easier to maintain**, and as they become second nature, you can gradually increase their intensity.

b. Make It Specific and Measurable

Vague habits are **hard to track** and easy to abandon. The more **specific** and **measurable** your habit is, the easier it will be to stay on course.

Instead of: "I'll eat healthier."

Say: "I'll add one serving of vegetables to my dinner each night."

When your habit has **clear parameters**, you'll know exactly what to do and when to do it.

c. Attach It to an Existing Habit

A great way to build a new habit is to **pair it with something you already do regularly**. This technique, known as **habit stacking**, helps integrate the new behavior naturally into your routine.

Example: "After I brush my teeth in the morning, I'll write down one thing I'm grateful for."

289

By linking your habit to an existing routine, you create a **cue** that reminds you to follow through.

d. Create a Reward System

Habits stick when they're **rewarding**. Your brain is wired to repeat behaviors that bring pleasure or a sense of accomplishment. **Celebrate small wins** to stay motivated and reinforce your new habit.

Example: After completing a week of your new habit, treat yourself to something enjoyable—like a good cup of coffee, a relaxing evening, or a new book.

Small rewards **strengthen positive reinforcement**, making it easier to maintain momentum.

e. Replace Bad Habits with Good Ones

It's not just about creating **new** habits—it's also about **eliminating bad ones**. The easiest way to break a bad habit is to **replace it with a positive alternative**.

Example: Instead of **scrolling social media before bed**, replace it with **reading a book** or practicing meditation.

Your **current habits—good or bad—are shaping your life**. By consciously **swapping negative habits for positive ones**, you take control of your daily routine and create a future that aligns with your goals.

The key to creating **purposeful** habits is **intentionality and consistency**. Start small, be specific, attach habits to existing routines, reward yourself, and replace negative behaviors with positive ones. Over time, these small actions will **reshape your life**, leading you toward the future you desire.

5. The Ripple Effect of Positive Habits

One of the most powerful aspects of habit formation is the **ripple effect**—one good habit often leads to others, creating a chain reaction of growth and improvement in multiple areas of your life. Small changes may seem insignificant in the moment, but over time, they set off a **domino effect** that leads to **big, long-term results**.

How One Habit Can Spark Transformation

Journaling each morning → Leads to better clarity and focus → Increases productivity → Improves decision-making.

Drinking more water → Encourages healthier food choices → Boosts energy levels → Enhances skin health.

Exercising for just 10 minutes a day → Increases energy → Improves sleep quality → Strengthens discipline and consistency in other areas.

Reading for 10-15 minutes daily → Expands knowledge → Improves critical thinking → Strengthens self-discipline and creativity.

Small actions **compound over time**, creating effortless momentum. **You don't need to change everything at once**—just **start with one habit**, and watch as it naturally influences other areas of your life.

Key Insight: Small Changes = Big Results

One tiny habit can reshape your entire lifestyle. By making small, intentional choices each day, you set yourself on a path of continuous growth. The ripple effect ensures that even the **smallest changes today lead to massive transformations over time.**

Instead of trying to overhaul your life all at once, **focus on one habit and let the ripple effect take over.**

6. Short-Term vs. Long-Term Happiness

Most people **chase instant gratification**, prioritizing what feels good in the moment over what benefits them in the long run. But true **happiness and fulfillment** don't come from fleeting pleasures—they come from **discipline, consistency, and aligning your actions with your future goals**.

While short-term choices can bring immediate comfort, they often **delay or sabotage long-term success**. On the other hand, habits that require effort and discipline today lead to **lasting confidence, health, and fulfillment** in the future.

Examples of Short-Term vs. Long-Term Happiness

- **Short-term happiness:** Skipping a workout to relax.
  Long-term happiness: Sticking to a fitness habit and feeling stronger, healthier, and more confident over time.
- **Short-term happiness:** Ordering fast food because it's convenient.
  Long-term happiness: Preparing nutritious meals and feeling more energized, improving your overall well-being.
- **Short-term happiness:** Scrolling social media for hours instead of reading or learning something new.
  Long-term happiness: Investing in self-education and

personal growth, which opens doors to better opportunities and a more fulfilling life.

- **Short-term happiness:** Procrastinating on an important task to avoid discomfort. **Long-term happiness:** Taking action, building momentum, and experiencing the rewards of productivity and achievement.

True Fulfillment Comes from Future-Focused Decisions

Short-term happiness is **tempting,** but it often leads to regret or stagnation. Long-term happiness requires **choosing what's best for your future self, not just what feels good in the moment.** The more you build habits that support your long-term well-being, the more **fulfilled, confident, and in control of your life** you will feel.

Key Takeaway:

Your habits create your reality. Every choice you make is shaping your future—so choose habits that build a happy, purposeful life, not just for today but for years to come. **Long-term happiness is built one small habit at a time.**

7. Habits to Build a Life of Purpose

The life you create is a direct result of the habits you practice every day. **Small, intentional habits** can shape your mindset, health, growth, and relationships—helping you live with greater purpose and fulfillment. Here are some simple but powerful habits that can make a **big impact** over time:

For Your Mindset:

A strong mindset is the foundation of a purposeful life. These habits help cultivate gratitude, self-awareness, and mental clarity.

Write down three things you're grateful for each morning to start the day with a positive outlook.

Practice mindful breathing or meditation for 5 minutes a day to reduce stress and stay present.

End each day by reflecting on one thing you did well, reinforcing confidence and self-growth.

For Your Health:

Your physical well-being affects every other aspect of your life. Small changes lead to lasting health benefits.

Drink a glass of water before your morning coffee to hydrate your body and boost energy.

Take the stairs instead of the elevator whenever possible to increase daily movement effortlessly.

Prepare one homemade meal each week to develop better eating habits and nourish your body.

For Your Growth:

Personal growth is a lifelong journey. These habits help you continuously learn, improve, and step outside your comfort zone.

Read 10 pages of a book or listen to an educational podcast daily to expand your knowledge.

Write down one thing you learned each day to reinforce new insights and keep growing.

Take one action each week that pushes you out of your comfort zone to build resilience and confidence.

For Your Relationships:

Strong relationships bring joy, support, and meaning to life. These small habits can help nurture deeper connections.

Send one kind message to a friend or loved one each week to maintain meaningful connections.

Schedule quality time with someone you care about to strengthen bonds and create lasting memories.

Listen actively during conversations without interrupting to show respect and deepen understanding.

8. What to Do When You Fall Off Track

No matter how committed you are to building good habits, **life happens**. You might get busy, feel unmotivated, or simply forget. The important thing isn't that you slipped—it's how quickly you **bounce back**.

Many people fall into the trap of **all-or-nothing thinking**, believing that one mistake means total failure. But in reality, progress is never linear. **It's not about being perfect—it's about staying consistent over time.**

Here's how to recover and get back on track **without guilt or frustration:**

Steps to Recover:
a. Acknowledge the Slip

Instead of beating yourself up, recognize that **setbacks are normal**. Every successful person has fallen off track at some point. What matters is **not staying stuck** in self-blame.

Wrong mindset: *"I missed a workout this week... I've failed, so I might as well give up."*

Better mindset: *"I missed a workout, but that doesn't define my progress. I'll start again today."*

b. Revisit Your Why

When motivation fades, your **why** is what will keep you going. Ask yourself:

- **Why did I start this habit in the first place?**
- **What long-term benefit does this bring me?**
- **How will my future self thank me for sticking with it?**

Reminding yourself of the **bigger picture** helps reignite your commitment.

c. Start Small Again

If getting back on track feels overwhelming, **reset with small steps.** You don't have to jump back in at full intensity—just focus on regaining **momentum.**

Missed a week of workouts? Start with just 5 minutes today.

Stopped reading daily? Pick up a book and read one page.

Dropped your journaling habit? Write one sentence to restart.

Small wins **build confidence** and help you ease back into the habit.

Progress Isn't Linear—But Consistency Wins

Success isn't about **never slipping up**—it's about **always coming back.** The people who succeed aren't the ones who never fail; they're the ones who **refuse to quit.**

Every time you **restart**, you prove to yourself that you're resilient. So don't focus on the slip—**focus on the comeback.**

Reflection Exercise:

Pick ONE habit to start today that aligns with your goals. **Commit to doing it for 21 days** to make it a habit, and **90 days** to make it part of your identity.

Watch how it transforms not just your routine, but your entire life.

The life you want **doesn't start someday—it starts today** with the habits you choose to build. **Small steps, taken consistently, lead to big results.**

Final Thoughts: Small Habits, Big Results

Building a life of purpose doesn't require **huge, dramatic changes**—it's about **small, intentional steps** taken **consistently** over time. Every great achievement, every major transformation, and every fulfilling life is built on **simple daily actions that compound over time.**

Chapter 23: Living in Alignment with Your Values

Living with purpose begins with understanding your **core values**—the guiding principles that shape your decisions, influence your actions, and define your vision for life. Your values are the foundation of who you are and what truly matters to you. When your daily choices align with these values, life feels **authentic, meaningful, and fulfilling**. But when your actions contradict them, you may experience **frustration, dissatisfaction, or a sense of disconnection** from yourself.

In a world filled with distractions, societal expectations, and external pressures, it's easy to lose sight of what's truly important. Many people chase success, approval, or security without realizing that fulfillment comes from living **in alignment with their inner truth**, not external validation.

When you live **in alignment with your values**, you experience **inner peace, clarity, and an unshakable sense of self.** Your life starts to feel more intentional, and every step you take moves you closer to the life you're meant to live.

1. What Are Values and Why Do They Matter?

Your **values** are the deeply held beliefs that define **what's important to you**. They shape your **identity**, influence your **choices**, and determine **how you navigate life**—from relationships and career to personal growth and everyday decisions.

When your actions align with your values, life feels **authentic, purposeful, and fulfilling**. But when you ignore or compromise your values, you may experience **inner conflict, dissatisfaction, and a lack of direction.**

Why Values Matter:
They give your life direction and meaning.
Knowing your values helps you set goals and make decisions that feel right for you, rather than just going with the flow.
They help you make decisions with clarity and confidence.
When faced with a difficult choice, your values act as a filter, guiding you toward the right path.
They serve as a compass, guiding you back to yourself when you feel lost or uncertain.
Whenever life feels overwhelming, reconnecting with your core values helps you realign with what truly matters.
They create inner peace by ensuring your actions reflect who you truly are.
When your daily life aligns with your values, you experience less stress, regret, and confusion—because you're living in a way that feels **true to you.**

Without Clear Values, You Might Find Yourself:
Making choices based on external pressures. You follow societal norms or other people's expectations instead of listening to your own needs.
Feeling unfulfilled or disconnected from your daily life. Your routine feels meaningless, and you struggle to find motivation or passion.

Frequently feeling resentful, drained, or overwhelmed.
You say "yes" to things that don't align with you, leading to exhaustion and frustration.

Making decisions that please others but leave you unsatisfied.
You prioritize what others want over what truly makes you happy, leading to regret.

Going through the motions without a sense of purpose.
You feel stuck in autopilot mode, unsure of what you really want or why you're doing what you're doing.

Reclaiming Control Through Your Values

When you **identify and prioritize your values**, you take control of your life. You stop making choices based on **fear, obligation, or habit** and start living with **intentionality, purpose, and fulfillment**.

Living in alignment with your values means that every action, big or small, supports the life you want to create. It's about choosing **what's right for you**, even when it's difficult or goes against the expectations of others. And ultimately, **it's the key to a life that feels deeply meaningful and true to who you are**.

2. Identifying Your Core Values

Before you can live in **alignment** with your values, you need to **define them**. If you've never intentionally explored your values, you're not alone—**most people haven't!** But once you do, it will **transform how you make decisions**, strengthen your sense of self, and help you **build a life that reflects who you truly are**.

Your values act as your **personal GPS**, guiding your choices, relationships, and priorities. When you know what you stand for, you stop living on autopilot and start making decisions that bring you **fulfillment and purpose**.

Reflection Exercise: Discovering Your Core Values

To uncover what truly matters to you, take some time to reflect on the following:

a. What Matters Most to You?

Think about moments in your life when you felt happiest, most fulfilled, or deeply at peace.

What was happening?

Who were you with?

What values were being honored? (Examples: **Love, creativity, growth, freedom, adventure**)

Example: If you felt happiest when traveling and experiencing new cultures, **freedom, exploration, and curiosity** might be core values for you.

b. What Do You Stand For?

Consider the principles that are **non-negotiable** for you. These are the things you deeply believe in and **would never compromise on.**

What are your strongest beliefs?

What qualities do you admire in others?

What values shape your decisions?

Examples of Core Values:

- **Integrity** – Always doing the right thing, even when no one is watching.
- **Honesty** – Being truthful and transparent in all situations.
- **Loyalty** – Standing by those you care about and keeping your commitments.
- **Ambition** – Striving for growth, success, and personal achievement.
- **Kindness** – Treating others with compassion and understanding.
- **Independence** – Valuing self-sufficiency and freedom.

c. What Makes You Feel Uncomfortable?

Often, the things that **bother you the most** can reveal the values that matter most to you. Think about moments that made you feel uneasy, resentful, or frustrated.

- **Did you feel disrespected?** (*Value: Respect*)
- **Did you feel like your time was wasted?** (*Value: Efficiency*)
- **Did you feel unseen or unheard?** (*Value: Connection*)
- **Did you feel controlled or restricted?** (*Value: Freedom*)

Example: If you often feel drained in environments where people are dishonest or manipulative, it may mean that **honesty and authenticity** are core values for you.

d. Narrow It Down: Your 3-5 Core Values

From your reflections, **choose 3-5 core values** that resonate **most deeply** with you. These are the **principles you want to live by every single day**.

Example Core Values:

- **Growth** – Always learning, evolving, and striving to become better.
- **Freedom** – Living life on your own terms, without unnecessary restrictions.
- **Connection** – Building meaningful relationships and deep emotional bonds.
- **Integrity** – Staying true to your word and moral principles.
- **Creativity** – Expressing yourself and thinking outside the box.

Identifying your core values is the **first step toward a life of authenticity and fulfillment.** When you live in alignment with your values, **decision-making becomes easier, relationships become more meaningful, and your life feels more purposeful.**

3. Aligning Your Actions with Your Values

It's one thing to **know** your values, but it's another to **live by them.** True alignment happens when your **daily actions reflect your core beliefs.** If there's a disconnect between what you value and how you live, you may feel unfulfilled, frustrated, or stuck.

Aligning your life with your values isn't about perfection—it's about making intentional choices that **support who you are and what truly matters to you.**

Steps to Align Your Life with Your Values
a. Assess Your Current Life

Before making changes, take an honest look at your current routines and choices.

Ask yourself:

- Are my daily actions in sync with my values?
- Are there areas where I feel out of alignment?
- Am I prioritizing what matters, or am I making choices based on obligation or habit?

Example:

If one of your core values is **family**, but you rarely spend time with loved ones because of work, there's a disconnect. **To realign**, you might decide to set boundaries around your work schedule and prioritize meaningful interactions with family.

b. Set Clear Intentions

Once you identify where you're **out of alignment**, set **clear, actionable intentions** to shift toward what matters.

Example:

If **health** is a core value, but you rarely prioritize movement or nourishing meals, an intention could be:

"I will prepare a nourishing meal for myself at least four times a week."

"I will go for a 15-minute walk every morning."

Intentions help **bridge the gap between values and actions**, making it easier to create a **life that feels right**.

c. Make Value-Based Decisions

Every choice you make either brings you **closer to** or **further from** the life you want. Before making a decision, **pause and ask yourself:**

✓ "Does this align with my values?"

✓ "Will this bring me closer to the life I want to create?"

If the answer is **no**, consider an alternative choice that **honors your values**.

Example:

If you value **growth and learning**, but you're spending hours scrolling social media instead of reading, you might decide to set limits on screen time and prioritize educational content.

d. Create Boundaries

Not everything—or everyone—will align with your values, and **that's okay**. Protect what matters to you by setting **healthy boundaries** around people, activities, or situations that **conflict with your values**.

Example:

If **peace** is a core value, you might decide to:

- Limit interactions with **negative, drama-filled environments.**
- Decline invitations to **events that drain your energy.**
- Spend more time in **calm, uplifting spaces** that make you feel good.

Boundaries aren't about shutting people out—they're about **prioritizing what supports your well-being**.

Living in alignment with your values means making **conscious choices** that reflect what truly matters to you. When your actions, decisions, and boundaries honor your values, you'll feel **more at peace, fulfilled, and in control of your life.**

Every small shift toward alignment brings you closer to the life you're meant to live.

4. Staying True to Yourself in a Noisy World

Living in alignment with your values isn't always easy—especially when **family, society, or peers have different expectations**. The world is full of **external influences** telling you who you should be, what you should do, and how you should live. But **staying true to yourself** is the key to a **fulfilling, purpose-driven life**.

When you honor your values despite outside pressures, you **build self-trust, confidence, and inner peace**. You stop living for approval and start living for **your own truth**.

Tips for Staying True to Yourself:
Trust Your Inner Compass
Your values are **personal**—they don't need to match anyone else's. What's right for someone else **may not be right for you**, and that's okay. Learn to trust your **own instincts** over societal expectations.

Example: If financial security is a core value, you might prioritize saving and building stability—even if your peers are focused on luxury purchases and short-term gratification.

Say No Without Guilt
Saying **no** to what doesn't align with your values is really saying **yes** to what does. People may not always understand your choices, but that doesn't mean you should compromise what's important to you.

Example: If health is a core value, you might decline late-night outings that interfere with your sleep or well-being. If peace is a core value, you might step away from toxic conversations or drama.

Saying **no** is a form of self-respect. The more you practice it, the **easier it becomes**.

Surround Yourself with Support

The people you spend time with **affect your mindset, choices, and overall well-being**. Surround yourself with those who **respect, support, and uplift your values**—not those who pressure you to conform.

Example: If personal growth is a core value, being around **motivated, open-minded individuals** will reinforce that mindset. If creativity is a value, connecting with **inspiring, artistic people** will help fuel your passion.

Seek out relationships that **energize you**, not ones that make you feel like you have to constantly explain or defend yourself.

Limit Comparison

Your **journey is unique**—it's not meant to look like anyone else's. Comparing yourself to others can lead you away from your own values and toward **external validation** that doesn't truly fulfill you.

Example: Just because society glorifies hustle culture doesn't mean you have to **sacrifice balance** if that's one of your values. Just because others define success by material wealth doesn't mean **you have to measure yourself the same way**.

Instead of asking, *"Am I doing what others expect?"*, ask:

✓ *"Am I living in a way that feels right for me?"*

✓ *"Does this align with my values and vision?"*

Staying true to yourself in a noisy world **takes courage**, but the reward is **a life that feels genuinely fulfilling**. When you follow your own path—guided by your **values, not external noise**—you experience more **clarity, confidence, and peace**.

The more you honor your values, the more your life will feel like your own.

5. The Benefits of Living in Alignment

When your **actions align with your values**, you'll notice profound changes in your life. Living authentically brings **clarity, confidence, and fulfillment**—you no longer feel like you're just going through the motions. Instead, your life starts to feel **purposeful and energizing**.

What Happens When You Live in Alignment?

Clarity: You'll make decisions with ease, knowing they align with your purpose and priorities. No more second-guessing or feeling lost.

Confidence: Living authentically makes you feel **secure in yourself** because you're no longer trying to fit into someone else's mold.

Fulfillment: Every day feels **more meaningful** when you honor your values. You wake up with a sense of direction rather than feeling stuck in autopilot.

Resilience: When challenges arise, you navigate them with **greater strength and intention** because your actions are rooted in something deeper than temporary emotions.

Real-Life Example: Living In vs. Out of Alignment

Imagine your **core values** are **growth, freedom, and creativity**.

Out of Alignment:

- You're in a job that stifles your creativity and offers no room for personal growth.

- You feel **stuck, unmotivated, and drained** because your daily routine doesn't reflect what truly matters to you.

- You prioritize security over personal fulfillment, and over time, you start to feel disconnected from yourself.

In Alignment:

- You **pursue a career or hobby** that allows you to express creativity and learn new skills.

- You set **boundaries** to ensure you have time for personal growth—whether through reading, learning, or exploring new opportunities.

- You feel **inspired and energized** because your daily actions reflect your true values.

Outcome: Living in alignment reignites your **passion for life**, brings a deeper sense of purpose, and makes even everyday tasks feel **meaningful and rewarding**.

When your choices align with your values, life feels **easier, more fulfilling, and more authentic**. You stop chasing what others expect and start building a life that genuinely **feels right for you**.

6. Reflection Exercise: Align Your Life

Self-awareness is the first step toward transformation. This **reflection exercise** will help you identify areas of misalignment, set clear intentions, and celebrate the moments when you've lived true to your values.

a. Identify Misalignment

Take a moment to reflect on your life.

- **Is there an area where your actions don't fully reflect your values?**
- **What part of your life feels off-balance?** (Work, relationships, health, personal growth?)
- **Which of your values is being neglected or compromise?**
- **How does this misalignment make you feel?**

Example: If one of your core values is **health**, but you frequently skip meals or neglect exercise due to a busy schedule, there's a disconnect.

b. Set an Intention

Once you've identified an area of misalignment, set **one small, actionable step** to realign yourself with your values. The key is to **start small** and build from there.

- **What's one simple action you can take today?**
- **How can you incorporate this value into your daily routine?**

Example:

- If your value is **health**, an intention could be:
  "I will prepare a nourishing meal tonight instead of ordering takeout."
  "I will go for a short walk during my lunch break."

- If your value is **connection**, an intention could be: "I will call a loved one today for a meaningful conversation."

c. Celebrate Alignment

Think about a time when you made a decision that fully aligned with your values.

- **What was the situation?**
- **Which of your values were honored?**
- **How did it make you feel?**

Example: If **growth** is a core value, you might recall a time when you stepped out of your comfort zone to take on a new challenge. You likely felt **proud, empowered, and in control of your life**—because you were acting in alignment with what matters most.

Final Thought:

Aligning your life with your values **doesn't require drastic change**—it starts with **small, intentional actions** every day. The more you make decisions that reflect who you truly are, the more **fulfilling and meaningful** your life will feel. **Your values are your guide—let them shape the life you create.**

Chapter 24: Finding Your Flow – Unlocking Peak Creativity and Productivity

We've all experienced those **magical moments** where we're so deeply immersed in a task that **time seems to disappear**. Whether it's **writing, painting, playing music, coding, problem-solving, or even exercising**, everything just **clicks**—our thoughts are sharp, our actions feel effortless, and we're **fully engaged** in the moment.

This powerful state is called **flow**—a mental zone where **productivity, creativity, and fulfillment** happen effortlessly. It's where **you do your best work, generate your best ideas, and feel the most alive**.

But flow isn't just about work—it's about **aligning your mind, body, and energy** so that whatever you do, whether in your **career, hobbies, or daily tasks**, feels **meaningful and engaging**.

1. What is the Flow State?

Flow state, also known as being **"in the zone,"** is a mental state of **complete absorption** in an activity. It's when your **mind and body work seamlessly together**, distractions fade into the background, and you're fully engaged in what you're doing.

Flow isn't just about **working harder**—it's about working in a way that feels **effortless and deeply satisfying**. When you're in flow, you're **not forcing productivity**—you're naturally **tapped into your best performance**.

Characteristics of Flow:

- **Total Focus:** You're completely immersed in the task, with no mental clutter.

- **Effortless Action:** Everything feels smooth and natural—like you're in sync with the work.

- **Distorted Sense of Time:** Hours can feel like minutes, as if time speeds up or slows down.

- **Loss of Self-Consciousness:** You're not second-guessing yourself—you're just **doing**.

- **A Sense of Control:** Even when the task is challenging, you feel **in charge of the moment**.

Why Flow Matters:

Boosts Creativity and Problem-Solving – Flow allows your mind to **think freely**, leading to breakthroughs and fresh ideas.

Increases Productivity and Efficiency – You get more done in less time because you're **fully engaged and focused**.

Enhances Emotional Well-Being – Flow naturally reduces stress and creates a sense of **inner peace**.

Creates a Sense of Purpose and Fulfillment – Engaging in meaningful work feels **deeply rewarding**, reinforcing motivation.

Flow: The Sweet Spot Between Boredom and Anxiety

Flow happens when a task is **challenging enough to engage you** but **not so overwhelming that it causes stress**.

If a task is too easy → You'll feel bored and disengaged. **If a task is too difficult** → You'll feel anxious and frustrated. **Flow happens when** → The challenge is **just right**—demanding enough to be engaging, but achievable enough to keep you going.

Flow isn't just a productivity hack—it's a **path to doing your best work, feeling more present, and living with greater fulfillment**. When you understand how to enter and maintain flow, you unlock a **new level of creativity, focus, and enjoyment** in everything you do.

2. The Science of Flow

Flow isn't just a **feeling**—it's a **neurological state** where your brain functions at **peak performance**. When you enter flow, your brain chemistry shifts, releasing powerful **neurotransmitters** that enhance focus, creativity, and motivation.

The Brain Chemicals Behind Flow

- **Dopamine** – Enhances **motivation, learning, and focus** by rewarding progress.
- **Norepinephrine** – Boosts **alertness and energy**, keeping you engaged.
- **Endorphins** – Reduce pain and create a sense of **euphoria and well-being**.
- **Anandamide** – Increases **lateral thinking**, helping you make unique connections and creative breakthroughs.

These **neurochemicals work together** to put your brain into an **optimal state of performance**, allowing you to work more efficiently, solve problems faster, and feel deeply engaged.

How Flow Impacts Your Brain:

Time Feels Distorted – Your brain filters out distractions and unnecessary details, making hours feel like minutes. **Your Inner Critic Goes Silent** – Self-doubt and overthinking fade away, allowing you to act with confidence and creativity. **You Access Deeper Learning** – Information is processed more efficiently, **improving memory, skill development, and problem-solving.**

The Benefits of Flow:

✓ **Improved Performance** – Athletes, artists, and entrepreneurs all use flow to **maximize their abilities** and produce their best work.

✓ **Enhanced Satisfaction** – Work feels more **meaningful, rewarding, and enjoyable** when you're fully engaged.

✓ **Reduced Stress and Anxiety** – Being **fully present in the moment** calms the mind and reduces worry.

Why This Matters:

When you **intentionally cultivate flow**, you unlock **peak performance, creativity, and fulfillment.** Flow isn't just about getting more done—it's about **doing better work, feeling more inspired, and enjoying the process.**

Understanding the science of flow allows you to harness its power—not just for productivity, but for a richer, more meaningful life.

3. How to Get Into Flow

Flow **doesn't happen by accident**—it's a state you **intentionally create** by setting up the right conditions. When you optimize your environment, choose the right tasks, and work with your natural rhythm, you can enter **flow more easily and more often**. Here's how:

a. Set the Right Environment

Minimize distractions – Turn off notifications, silence your phone, and eliminate anything that might pull your focus away.

Create an inspiring workspace – A well-lit, comfortable, and clutter-free space helps boost concentration and creativity.

Use background noise intentionally – Some people work best in silence, while others focus better with instrumental music, white noise, or nature sounds. Experiment to find what works best for you.

b. Choose a Challenging but Doable Task

Flow happens when a task is difficult enough to engage you but not so hard that it feels overwhelming.

- **Too easy?** Add a challenge – Set a time limit, increase the difficulty, or aim for a personal best.
- **Too hard?** Break it into smaller, manageable steps – This reduces mental resistance and makes progress feel more achievable.

Example: If you're writing, instead of aiming to finish an entire article, focus on writing **just one paragraph**. Once you start, momentum will carry you forward.

c. Find Your Rhythm

Identify your most productive hours – Are you a **morning person, night owl, or do you thrive in the afternoon?** Work with your **natural energy**, not against it.

Time-block your focus sessions – Dedicate **specific periods** for deep work, free from distractions. Set clear start and end times to build consistency.

Example: If you're most productive in the morning, schedule deep work before noon and save less demanding tasks (emails, meetings, errands) for later.

d. Embrace Deep Work

Stop multitasking – Flow requires **single-tasking—fully committing to one thing at a time**. Jumping between tasks breaks concentration and prevents deep engagement. **Try the Pomodoro Method** – Work for **25 minutes**, then take a **5-minute break**. Repeat until you hit peak focus. Longer sessions (50-90 minutes) with longer breaks can also be effective.

Example: Instead of checking your phone every few minutes, **set a timer for 45 minutes of focused work**, then reward yourself with a 10-minute break.

Flow isn't something you wait for—it's something you **actively cultivate**. When you **control your environment, choose the right challenges, and structure your time effectively**, you make it easier to **tap into flow on demand**.

The more you practice getting into flow, the more natural and effortless it becomes.

4. Flow and Inspiration

Flow isn't just about getting things done—it's about **unlocking your highest creative potential**. When you're in flow, inspiration comes **naturally**, ideas connect effortlessly, and creativity feels **limitless**.

How Flow Fuels Creativity

Your mind connects ideas more freely – In flow, your brain links concepts in ways you wouldn't normally see, leading to breakthroughs and deeper insights.

Artists, writers, and musicians experience their best work in flow – When fully immersed in the creative process, self-doubt fades, and expression feels effortless.

Innovation happens when you stop overthinking – Flow removes mental resistance, allowing ideas to come naturally instead of forcing creativity.

Example: A writer experiencing flow may produce **pages of work effortlessly**, while a musician might compose an entire piece in a single session—completely absorbed in their craft.

How Flow Feels Like Alignment

Flow isn't just about **productivity**—it's about feeling **deeply connected** to your work and purpose.

✓ **You feel completely in sync with what you're doing.** There's no resistance—only **engagement and excitement**.

✓ **Work becomes effortless and enjoyable.** Instead of struggling, you **glide through the process**, fully present in the moment.

✓ **You experience fulfillment and joy in the process itself.** Success isn't just about the **end result**—it's about how rewarding the journey feels.

Example: A painter lost in their work isn't **thinking about how many hours have passed**—they're simply **enjoying the act of creation**.

Flow is **more than a state of focus**—it's a space where **passion, inspiration, and purpose come together**. Whether you're creating, problem-solving, or building something meaningful, flow allows you to **operate at your highest level** while feeling deeply fulfilled.

When you embrace flow, creativity becomes effortless, and your work becomes an extension of who you are.

5. Maintaining Flow in a Distracted World

Flow is **powerful**, but in today's world, distractions are everywhere—notifications, emails, endless scrolling, and interruptions constantly pull us out of deep focus. **Staying in the zone requires intention and discipline.** Here's how to protect and maintain your flow state:

Identify Your Biggest Distractions

First, pinpoint what **breaks your focus the most** so you can set up defenses against it.

- **Is it social media?** Use app blockers or set specific "no-phone" times.
- **Is it emails or messages?** Turn off notifications and schedule check-ins at specific times.

- **Is it background noise?** Use noise-canceling headphones or listen to instrumental music to stay in the zone.

Action Step: Make a list of your **top 3 distractions** and create a strategy to **reduce or eliminate them** during flow sessions.

Schedule Uninterrupted Time

Protect your **flow state** by setting **dedicated time blocks** for deep, focused work.

Use time-blocking: Set specific hours where you focus on one task with no interruptions.

Communicate boundaries: Let others know when you're in deep work mode to avoid unnecessary interruptions.

Batch similar tasks together: Instead of switching between different tasks, group similar activities to maintain momentum.

Example: If mornings are your most productive time, **block 9 AM - 12 PM** for deep work, and save emails and calls for later.

Create a Pre-Flow Ritual

A **pre-flow ritual** helps you transition into deep focus by **resetting your mind and signaling to your brain that it's time to work.**

- **Breathing exercises** – A few deep breaths can calm your mind and improve focus.
- **Journaling or brain-dumping** – Clear mental clutter by writing down thoughts before starting your task.
- **Stretching or light movement** – Loosen up your body to prevent restlessness.

- **Listening to a specific playlist or ambient sound** – Condition your brain to associate certain sounds with deep work mode.

Example: Before diving into creative work, take **five deep breaths, stretch for two minutes, and put on your "flow state" playlist.**

Distractions are **everywhere**, but with the right **systems and habits**, you can **protect your flow state** and **stay deeply immersed in meaningful work.**

6. Flow State in Daily Life

Flow **isn't just for work**—it can be a part of **every area of life**, turning routine activities into **engaging and fulfilling experiences**. Whether you're working, creating, or moving your body, flow brings **joy, presence, and peak performance** into the moment.

At Work: Finding Flow in Productivity

✓ **Focus on meaningful projects** that challenge and excite you— flow thrives in tasks that stretch your abilities but remain achievable.

✓ **Make routine tasks more engaging**—add a time challenge, create a reward system, or batch similar tasks to keep momentum going.

✓ **Eliminate distractions**—protect your deep work time so you can fully immerse yourself.

Example: A designer might experience flow when creating a new visual concept, completely absorbed in colors, layout, and innovation.

In Personal Life: Flow Through Creativity

✓ **Engage in hobbies** that allow for deep immersion—painting, writing, music, gardening, or even DIY projects.

✓ **Add mindfulness to everyday tasks**—turn activities like **cooking, cleaning, or organizing** into flow moments by **being fully present** instead of rushing through them.

✓ **Limit external noise**—disconnect from distractions and let yourself **fully enjoy the process.**

Example: A musician playing an instrument may lose track of time, completely immersed in the rhythm and melody of their music.

In Physical Activities: Flow in Movement

✓ **Exercise can create deep flow states**—whether you're lifting weights, running, doing yoga, or practicing a sport, movement becomes effortless and rhythmic.

✓ **Sync mind and body**—pay attention to how your body moves and breathes, creating a natural rhythm.

✓ **Challenge yourself but keep it enjoyable**—flow happens when the **difficulty level keeps you engaged without feeling overwhelmed.**

Example: A runner hitting their stride experiences a **"runner's high,"** where movement feels **effortless, the mind is clear, and focus is razor-sharp.**

7. Recognizing When You're Out of Flow

Even with the right setup, **flow isn't always easy to access.** Some days, distractions win. Other times, your mind feels scattered, and focus seems impossible. **Recognizing when you're out of flow is the first step to getting back into it.**

Signs of Resistance: When Flow Feels Out of Reach
- **Feeling stuck, distracted, or unmotivated** – Your mind keeps wandering, and getting started feels like a struggle
- **Overanalyzing and second-guessing yourself** – You're caught in self-doubt, making it hard to take action.
- **Constantly switching between tasks** – Instead of making progress, you jump from one thing to another without deep focus.

Example: A writer trying to finish an article keeps **editing the same sentence over and over**, instead of letting ideas flow.

How to Get Back Into Flow:
- **Take a Break** – Sometimes, **stepping away is the best way forward**. Reset your energy with:
  A **quick walk** outside to clear your mind.
- **Deep breathing or meditation** to reset your focus.
- **Listening to music** or engaging in a short, enjoyable activity before diving back in.
- **Revisit Your "Why"** – Ask yourself:
  ✓ *Why does this task matter?*
  ✓ *What impact will it have?*
  ✓ *How will I feel once it's done?*

Reconnecting with your **purpose** behind the work reignites **motivation and engagement.**

Example: If you're struggling to complete a project, remind yourself **how finishing it will bring value**—whether it's personal growth, career advancement, or simply the satisfaction of completing something important.

- **Adjust Your Challenge Level** – Flow thrives between **boredom and anxiety**.

  If you're struggling:

  ✓ **Too easy?** Increase the challenge—set a **time limit, add creativity, or raise the difficulty**.

  ✓ **Too hard?** Break it into **smaller, manageable steps** to make progress feel achievable.

Example: If a musician feels uninspired practicing scales, they might switch to **learning a new, slightly more difficult song** to re-engage their mind.

Your Flow Challenge:

Identify one task or activity where you'd love to experience flow more often.

Apply one strategy from this chapter to create better conditions for deep focus.

Reflect: What changes do you notice when you work in flow? How does it impact your creativity, efficiency, and overall well-being?

Final Thought:

The more you cultivate flow, the more you unlock your highest potential—creatively, productively, and emotionally.

Find your rhythm, eliminate distractions, and let yourself step fully into the zone.

Chapter 25: Mind Your Business & Trust the Process

In a world full of distractions, it's easy to get caught up in **what everyone else is doing**—watching their moves, comparing progress, and questioning your own path. But real success comes when you **stay in your lane, focus on your own journey, and trust the process**.

Why Staying in Your Lane is Key to Real Success – The moment you shift your focus to others, you lose momentum in your own life. Growth happens when you **mind your business and focus on your own work**.

The Danger of Distraction – Watching others too much can make you **doubt yourself, slow down your progress, and lose sight of your goals**. Comparison creates unnecessary pressure, but when you trust your own path, you move forward with confidence.

How Trusting the Process Leads to Long-Term Success & Peace – Growth isn't always instant, and success doesn't happen overnight. **Patience, discipline, and belief in your journey** will take you further than chasing quick results or comparing timelines.

1. Patience is a Virtue

In a world obsessed with **instant success**, it's easy to feel like you're falling behind. But true success isn't about rushing—it's about **trusting the timing of your life**. Everything unfolds when it's meant to, and learning to be **patient with your journey** is one of the greatest skills you can develop.

Understanding Divine Timing: Your Season Will Come

Not everything happens when you **want** it to, but it always happens when you're **ready** for it. Just like seasons change in nature, life moves in **cycles**—and your **season of success, love, and abundance** will arrive when the time is right.

Example: A tree doesn't rush to grow. It takes **years of steady growth underground** before it flourishes. Your journey is no different. **The foundation you're building now is what will support your future success.**

The Difference Between Delayed Success and Failure

Just because something **hasn't happened yet** doesn't mean it **won't happen at all.** Many people mistake **delayed success** for failure and give up right before their breakthrough.

- **Delayed Success = Growth in Progress** – The time you spend learning, building, and evolving is preparing you for success.
- **Failure = Stopping Before You Reach It** – The only true failure is quitting before your time comes.

Example: Think of every major success story—most people had years of unseen hard work before they finally "made it." The ones who **stayed patient and consistent** were the ones who reached their goals.

How Rushing or Forcing Things Can Backfire

When you try to **force success**, you often end up with **less than what you truly deserve**. Rushing leads to:

- **Burnout** – Moving too fast without a strong foundation can lead to exhaustion.

327

- **Poor Decisions** – Making choices out of desperation rather than strategy.
- **Short-Term Wins, Long-Term Regret** – Cutting corners may bring quick success, but it's not sustainable.

Example: A rushed relationship, business deal, or career move might seem exciting at first, but if it's not built on **real alignment and preparation**, it can fall apart just as quickly.

Be Genuinely Happy for Others, Knowing Your Time is Coming

A major sign of **trusting the process** is **celebrating others' wins** without feeling jealous or discouraged.

✓ **Their success doesn't take away from yours.** There's room for **everyone** to win.

✓ **Use others' success as motivation, not comparison.** If it happened for them, it means it's **possible for you too**.

✓ **Your journey is unique.** What's meant for you **will never miss you**—it's just taking the time it needs.

Mindset Shift: Instead of thinking, *"Why not me?"*, say, *"If it's happening for them, I know my time is coming too."*

2. Comparison is the Thief of Joy

One of the quickest ways to **drain your energy and kill your motivation** is by constantly comparing yourself to others. **When you focus too much on someone else's journey, you lose sight of your own.**

The Dangers of Constantly Watching Others & Feeling Behind

It's easy to feel like you're **not doing enough** when you see other people hitting milestones—getting promotions, launching businesses, traveling, or achieving success.

But here's the truth: **Your timeline is YOURS.** Just because someone else is succeeding now doesn't mean you're failing.

Example: Two people can plant seeds at the same time, but one tree may grow faster than the other due to unseen factors. **Your growth is happening—even if you can't see it yet.**

When you compare too much, you risk:

- **Losing confidence in yourself** – You start questioning your progress instead of trusting your journey.
- **Wasting time and energy** – Instead of focusing on your own growth, you spend energy watching someone else's.
- **Making impulsive decisions** – You might rush into things before you're ready, just to "keep up."

Social Media's Illusion: People Only Show Their Wins, Not the Struggles

Social media **amplifies comparison** because most people **only post their highlights**, not the failures, struggles, or behind-the-scenes work it took to get there.

- **You see:** The vacation, the new house, the business launch.
- **You don't see:** The sleepless nights, the financial stress, the self-doubt, or the years of hard work behind the scenes.

Mindset Shift: Instead of thinking, *"They have it all together, and I don't,"* remind yourself: *"I'm seeing the finished product, not the process. I'm still in my process."*

The Difference Between Inspiration & Unhealthy Comparison

Comparison **isn't always bad**—it depends on how you use it.

Inspiration → Motivates you, expands your vision, and reminds you what's possible.

Unhealthy Comparison → Makes you feel inadequate, discouraged, and envious.

Ask Yourself:

✔ *"Does this motivate me to improve, or does it make me feel like I'm not enough?"*

✔ *"Am I using this as proof of what's possible, or as a reason to doubt myself?"*

If something **inspires you,** use it as fuel. But if it makes you feel **less than**, it's time to shift your focus back to your own lane.

Learning to Clap for Others Without Feeling Like You're Losing

A true sign of **confidence and trust in your journey** is being able to **celebrate others' success without feeling threatened.**

Why? Because someone else's win does NOT take away from yours. There's room for everyone to succeed.

Think abundance, not competition – There's more than enough success to go around.

Use their success as proof that it's possible for you too. Stay focused on your own journey – Your only competition is **who you were yesterday.**

Affirmation: "I am on my own timeline. Someone else's success doesn't take away from mine—if anything, it means my turn is coming."

3. Stay in Your Lane

One of the biggest keys to **success, peace, and long-term growth** is **focusing on your own journey instead of constantly looking sideways.** The moment you start worrying about what others are doing, you **lose momentum in your own lane.** True success comes from **staying focused, eliminating distractions, and trusting in your unique path.**

The Power of Focusing on Your Own Growth

When you're constantly checking on others, you waste **energy that could be used to improve yourself.** The real growth happens when you:

✓ **Track your OWN progress, not someone else's.**

✓ **Invest in developing your skills and mindset.**

✓ **Measure success based on YOUR goals, not society's standards.**

Example: Imagine a runner in a race. If they keep looking sideways at their competitors, they slow down, lose focus, and risk falling behind. **Winners focus straight ahead.**

Lesson? The more you focus on YOUR lane, the faster and further you go.

Avoiding Distractions & Unnecessary Competition

Not every opportunity, trend, or person deserves your attention. Unnecessary distractions can **derail your focus and slow your progress.**

Competing with others is a waste of time – The only person you should compete with is **who you were yesterday.**

Just because something works for someone else doesn't mean it's for you – Not all opportunities align with your purpose. **Stay mindful of where you put your energy** – If it's not helping you grow, it's holding you back.

Mindset Shift: Instead of thinking, *"I need to outdo them,"* shift to *"I need to outdo my past self."*

The Danger of Copying Others' Blueprints

What works for someone else may NOT work for you. When you try to follow someone else's exact path, you risk:

Losing your **own unique voice and vision.** Feeling **disconnected** from what truly fulfills you. Struggling with **inauthentic success** that doesn't even make you happy.

Example: A person trying to copy someone else's business strategy, creative style, or career path might achieve success, but if it **doesn't align with who they truly are**, they'll eventually feel **empty, frustrated, or stuck.**

Your journey is meant to be uniquely yours. You can learn from others, but **your path should be built around your own strengths, passions, and purpose.**

Why Authenticity is Your Biggest Advantage

Nobody can do what YOU do the way YOU do it. Your **experiences, perspective, and skills are unique**—and that's your **superpower.**

✓ **People connect with what's real.** The more authentic you are, the stronger your impact.

✓ **Success built on YOUR terms will always be more fulfilling** than success built on imitation.

✓ **Your individuality makes you irreplaceable.** Instead of trying to fit in, stand out by being **fully yourself.**

Affirmation: "No one can compete with me because no one else is me. My journey is mine, and I trust that it's unfolding exactly as it should."

4. Short-Term vs. Long-Term Happiness

One of the biggest obstacles to success is the **temptation of instant gratification**—wanting quick wins, fast results, and immediate rewards. But true fulfillment and success don't happen overnight. **They are built over time through patience, discipline, and long-term thinking.**

Let's break down the difference between **chasing short-term pleasure** and **building long-term success.**

The Trap of Instant Gratification

In today's fast-paced world, it's easy to want **immediate results**—whether it's money, validation, or success. But chasing **shortcuts and quick highs** often leads to **long-term dissatisfaction**.

- **Chasing quick wins** – Focusing on fast money, social media validation, or "hacks" instead of real growth.
- **Taking shortcuts** – Looking for an easy way instead of putting in the work.
- **Seeking external approval** – Needing recognition instead of focusing on what truly fulfills you.

Example: A person who jumps from one business idea to another, chasing fast success, never builds anything sustainable. Meanwhile, the person who **stays patient and consistent** eventually creates something solid and lasting.

The Danger of Impatience

- **Quitting too soon** – Many people give up right before their breakthrough.
- **Switching paths too often** – Constantly starting over instead of **sticking to one thing and mastering it.**
- **Losing sight of the bigger picture** – Getting discouraged because success isn't happening fast enough.

Mindset Shift: Instead of thinking, *"Why isn't this happening now?"*, shift to *"What I'm building takes time, and every step forward counts."*

The Power of Delayed Gratification

All **great achievements take time.** The most successful people understand that **real success isn't about quick wins—it's about long-term growth.**

✓ **Why the best things take time** – Mastery, financial freedom, strong relationships, and personal growth all require **consistent effort over years—not days.**

✓ **Focusing on lasting success instead of temporary highs** – A well-built foundation leads to success that actually **lasts.**

Examples of people who stayed the course and won big: Howard Schultz – Rejected by over **200 investors** before securing funding for Starbucks, transforming it into a global coffee empire.

Sara Blakely – Failed the LSAT twice and faced multiple rejections before launching Spanx with her savings, later becoming the **youngest self-made female billionaire.**

Colonel Sanders – At **65 years old**, after failing at multiple jobs, he pitched his KFC recipe and got rejected **over 1,000 times** before finding success.

Lesson? The people who stay **patient, consistent, and focused** are the ones who win **in the long run.**

Building a Foundation for Long-Term Fulfillment

If you want **real, lasting success**, you need to make **choices today that benefit your future self.**

How to make better choices now:

- **Prioritize long-term goals over temporary pleasure.**
- **Invest in yourself** – Learn, grow, and develop real skills.
- **Build something that lasts** – Whether it's a business, career, or personal development, focus on longevity.

The importance of discipline and consistency:

Success is built on **small, daily habits** that compound over time. **What you do consistently matters more than what you do occasionally.**

Why patience is key to real happiness and success:

When you **trust the process**, you remove unnecessary stress. You know that as long as you're doing the work, **your time will come.**

5. Trust the Process

Success **isn't an overnight event**—it's a journey built over time with **consistency, discipline, and patience.** The people who truly win in life are the ones who **stay committed even when they don't see immediate results.**

The problem? Many people give up **too soon** because they expect instant success. But when you **trust the process,** you realize that **every small effort, every lesson, and every setback is leading you somewhere greater.**

Success is Built Over Time, Not Overnight

Every great success story **started small**—no one reaches the top instantly.

The work you put in **today** is shaping your **tomorrow,** even if you don't see it yet.

Growth happens in the **unseen moments**—the late nights, the early mornings, the small wins that add up over time.

Example:

A musician who practices daily might not feel like they're improving immediately, but after months of consistent effort, their skills will be **on a whole new level.**

Lesson? The results will come—but only if you keep going.

Why Consistency, Discipline & Belief Matter More Than Shortcuts

Too many people **chase quick success,** looking for the easiest way instead of putting in the work. But here's the truth:

✓ **Consistency beats talent when talent isn't consistent.**

✓ Discipline keeps you going when motivation fades.

✓ Belief in yourself is what keeps you from quitting.

Example:

A business owner who stays **consistent** through slow seasons, learns from failures, and **keeps showing up** will eventually build something sustainable—while the person looking for fast money will burn out and start over repeatedly.

Success isn't about how fast you get there—it's about whether you're willing to stay the course.

Learning to Enjoy the Journey Instead of Just Chasing the Destination

One of the biggest mistakes people make is thinking **happiness only comes after success**—but if you don't learn to enjoy the process, you'll always be chasing something.

- Find joy in the **small wins**—every step forward is progress.
- Appreciate the **growth and lessons** along the way.
- Understand that **who you become on the journey is just as important as the goal itself.**

Example:

A fitness journey isn't just about **losing weight or hitting a number**—it's about feeling stronger, more confident, and disciplined. The daily commitment is what transforms you, not just the final result.

When you love the process, success becomes inevitable.

Signs You're on the Right Path (Even When It Doesn't Feel Like It)

Sometimes, you're making more progress than you realize. Here are **key signs you're growing, even if success isn't obvious yet:**

- **You're more focused and intentional** – You're taking your goals seriously and working toward them.
- **You're facing challenges but learning from them** – Struggles aren't setbacks; they're signs of growth.
- **You're improving, even if it's slow** – Small progress is still progress.
- **You no longer feel the need to compare yourself to others** – You're starting to trust your own journey.
- **You're committed even when it's hard** – The fact that you haven't quit means you're already ahead of most people.

Mindset Shift: Instead of thinking *"Why isn't this happening faster?"*, remind yourself *"Every step forward is bringing me closer. I am exactly where I need to be."*

6. The Bigger Picture

Every action, every challenge, and every lesson you're experiencing right now is preparing you for what's coming. Even when things don't make sense in the moment, there is a bigger picture unfolding.

The key to long-term success isn't just working hard—it's trusting that every step, every delay, and every lesson is leading you somewhere greater than you can even imagine.

Everything You Do Now is Preparing You for What's Coming

Success isn't just about what you achieve—it's about who you become along the way. Every skill you learn, every challenge you overcome, and every habit you build is shaping you into the person who's ready for the next level.

The **discipline** you develop today will make success easier to maintain later.

The **patience** you build now will help you handle bigger opportunities with grace. The **setbacks** you face will teach you resilience and wisdom for future challenges.

Example: Some of the greatest leaders, entrepreneurs, and artists spent years in preparation before their breakthrough. Every step mattered—even the ones that didn't seem important at the time.

Lesson? What you're doing now isn't wasted effort—it's the foundation for your future success.

How Setbacks, Detours, and Failures Are Part of the Process

It's easy to feel discouraged when things don't go as planned. But every successful person has faced setbacks—the difference is, they didn't quit.

- **Failures are lessons** – Every setback is teaching you something valuable.
- **Detours lead to unexpected opportunities** – What seems like a delay may actually be redirection to something better.
- **Struggles make success meaningful** – The journey is what gives success its true value.

Example: Steve Jobs was fired from his own company before coming back stronger and making Apple the global success it is today. His setback was actually the setup for his greatest achievements.

When things don't go as planned, remind yourself: The process is still working, even when it feels like it isn't.

Why Faith in Yourself and Your Vision is the Ultimate Key

At the end of the day, the people who succeed are the ones who believe in themselves—even when no one else does.

✓ Trust that your work will pay off.

✓ Trust that your timing is right.

✓ Trust that what's meant for you will never miss you.

Mindset Shift: Instead of asking, *"What if this doesn't work?"*, start saying, *"What if this turns out even better than I imagined?"*

Stay focused on your own journey.

Stop worrying about what others are doing.

Keep showing up, even when results aren't instant.

Because when you mind your business, trust the process, and stay consistent, success is inevitable.

Reflection Exercise: Focus, Patience & Trusting the Process

Step 1: Identify Your Own Path

- Write down your **biggest long-term goal**—the one that truly excites and fulfills you.

- Now, write down **three small actions** you can take this week to move closer to it.

- Ask yourself: *Am I focusing on these actions, or am I getting distracted by watching others?*

Step 2: Comparison Detox

- Think about a time you compared yourself to someone else and felt discouraged.
- Ask yourself:
- Was I seeing their full journey, or just their highlight reel?
- What could I learn from their success without feeling like I'm behind?
- What strengths do I have that make my path unique?

Step 3: Short-Term vs. Long-Term Thinking

- Write down one thing you do **for instant gratification** that doesn't serve your long-term success (e.g., scrolling for hours, procrastinating, chasing quick money).
- Now, write down **one long-term habit** you can replace it with (e.g., reading, learning, practicing your craft, investing in your health).
- Challenge yourself to commit to this change for **one week** and reflect on how it makes you feel.

Step 4: Patience & Trusting the Process

- Think about a past situation where you **rushed something** and later realized you should have waited.
- Now, think of a time where you **waited, stayed consistent, and it paid off.**
- What did these experiences teach you about trusting the process?

Final Thought:

Write down this affirmation and repeat it when you start feeling impatient:

"My time is coming. I trust my path. What's meant for me will not miss me."

Chapter 26: Protecting Your Energy – The Power of Positivity and Boundaries

Your energy is your **most valuable asset**—it affects your mindset, your productivity, your relationships, and your overall well-being. But in a world full of distractions, negativity, and outside influences, **protecting your energy is a skill you have to master.**

Not everyone and everything deserves access to your time, thoughts, and emotions. **Without strong boundaries, you can easily become drained, overwhelmed, and disconnected from your true self.** But when you learn to guard your energy, you take control of your life—you feel lighter, more focused, and more at peace.

1. The Energy You Surround Yourself With Matters

Your environment and the people you surround yourself with **directly affect your mindset, mood, and overall well-being.** You **can't live a positive, fulfilling life if you're constantly surrounded by negativity, drama, or draining energy.**

Every interaction either **charges your battery or drains it**—which is why you have to be intentional about **who and what you give your energy to.**

Energy is Contagious: Choose Wisely

Positive people uplift you – They inspire, support, and encourage growth.

Negative people drain you – They complain, criticize, and leave you feeling exhausted.

Example: Have you ever left a conversation **feeling lighter, more motivated, and excited?** That's high-vibrational energy. On the other hand, if you feel **drained, irritated, or anxious after being around someone**, that's a sign their energy is negatively impacting yours.

Lesson? Protect your space—don't allow just anyone access to your energy.

Your Environment Shapes Your Mindset

It's not just **people** that affect your energy—your **physical and digital environment** plays a huge role, too.

Your space matters – A cluttered, chaotic space can create mental overwhelm, while a clean, peaceful environment boosts clarity   and   focus.
Social media consumption – Are you following people who inspire you, or are you constantly absorbing negativity and comparison?
Work and social settings – Does your job or friend group leave you feeling fulfilled or emotionally drained?

Action Step: Pay attention to **how you feel** after being in certain places, watching certain content, or spending time with certain people. **If something consistently drains you, it's time to reevaluate your exposure to it.**

The Energy Audit: Who & What Deserves Access to You?

Ask yourself:

- Who makes me feel energized, inspired, and supported?
- Who constantly drains my energy, complains, or brings negativity into my space?

- What activities and environments uplift me vs. deplete me?

Your energy is too valuable to be wasted on things and people that **do not contribute to your growth, peace, and happiness.**

2. Recognizing Draining vs. Energizing Environments

Every space you enter carries **energy**—and that energy can either **fuel you or drain you**. Sometimes, you don't even realize the impact of an environment until you **step away and feel the difference.**

A simple rule to remember:

✓ **If you leave a space feeling energized, inspired, or motivated—it's good for you.**

If you leave feeling drained, frustrated, or heavy—it's not the right space for you.

Draining Environments: When Something Feels "Off"

Certain places and social settings can **pull your energy down** without you even realizing it.

- **Toxic Workplaces** – Office gossip, constant stress, and negativity can slowly wear you down.
- **Dysfunctional Friendships** – If every interaction feels forced, competitive, or full of drama, it's taking more than it's giving.
- **Chaotic, Cluttered Spaces** – A messy or disorganized environment can create mental fog and overwhelm.
- **Negative Social Media Feeds** – Constant exposure to toxic debates, bad news, and comparison culture affects your mindset.

345

Example: If you feel mentally exhausted after scrolling social media or spending time in a certain place, it's a **sign that environment is draining you.**

Energizing Environments: Spaces That Uplift & Inspire You

The best environments **fill you up, spark creativity, and encourage growth.**

✓ **Supportive Social Circles** – Surrounding yourself with people who celebrate your wins, challenge you to grow, and uplift your energy.

✓ **Calm & Organized Spaces** – A tidy, peaceful environment reduces stress and improves focus.

✓ **Creative or Growth-Focused Communities** – Places where people share ideas, collaborate, and push each other to be better.

✓ **Nature & Movement-Based Spaces** – Being in nature, exercising, or simply stepping outside can **instantly recharge your energy.**

Example: Think about a time you left a space feeling **refreshed, motivated, and excited about life**—that's a sign of an energizing environment.

The Silent Impact: How Environments Subtly Shift Your Mindset

Even if you think you're **immune to negativity**, constantly being in **low-energy environments** can:

Make you doubt yourself – Being around people who complain or criticize can lower your confidence.

Drain your motivation – If no one around you is working toward goals, it's easy to feel stagnant.

Shift your mood without you realizing it – Over time, negativity can become your "normal" if you stay in it long enough.

Mindset Shift: Instead of **adjusting to draining environments,** start seeking and creating spaces that **energize and inspire you.**

3. Handling Relationships with Negative People

Not everyone in your life is easily **removable**—some negative people may be family members, coworkers, or long-time friends. But just because they're present in your life doesn't mean their **negativity has to infiltrate your space.**

You **can't control other people,** but you *can* control **how much access they have to your energy.**

When Someone's Negativity Weighs You Down

Some people constantly:

- Complain about everything but never take action. See problems instead of solutions.
- Drain your excitement by projecting their own fears and doubts.
- Bring drama, gossip, or toxic energy into every conversation.

Example: You share a new idea with a friend, and instead of support, they list all the reasons why it won't work. Their negativity doesn't reflect reality—it reflects **their own mindset.**

Lesson? If someone's energy consistently **pulls you down,** it's time to **adjust your approach** to them.

Limit What You Share with Negative People

If you care about someone but **their negativity affects you**, you don't have to **share everything** with them.

- Omit details that could invite negativity.
- Don't seek validation from people who don't see your vision.
- Keep certain dreams and plans private until they're solid.

Example: If you're making big career moves or starting a new project, **avoid sharing it with someone who always doubts you.** Instead, talk to **people who uplift and encourage you.**

Energy Tip: Not everyone needs a front-row seat in your life. Some people are better loved from a distance.

Boundaries: Protecting Your Peace Without Cutting People Off

Boundaries aren't about **shutting people out**—they're about protecting your **mental and emotional space.**

- **Reduce unnecessary contact.** If you know someone's energy is draining, don't engage more than necessary.
- **Shift the conversation.** If they bring negativity, change the subject or disengage.
- **Decide what level of access they have to you.** You don't owe **everyone** deep conversations or personal details.

Example: A family member who constantly criticizes your decisions doesn't need to know every detail of your life. Keep conversations light and **redirect negative discussions.**

4. Choosing Who and What Gets Your Energy

Your **energy is sacred**—who and what you give it to **directly shapes your mindset, emotions, and future.** The people around you can either **elevate you** or **drain you**, and it's up to you to **choose wisely.**

If you want to live a **fulfilled, successful, and peaceful life**, you have to be **intentional about where your energy goes.**

Be Intentional About Your Inner Circle

Not everyone deserves **a front-row seat in your life**. Your inner circle should be filled with people who:

✓ **Encourage you when things get tough.**

✓ **Support your growth without feeling threatened.**

✓ **Celebrate your wins without jealousy or judgment.**

✓ **Bring positive energy into your life.**

Example: If you leave a conversation **feeling lighter, inspired, or motivated**, that's a sign you're around the right people. If you leave feeling **drained, frustrated, or doubting yourself**, it's time to reevaluate that connection.

Energy Check: Ask yourself, *"Do the people around me make me feel more alive, or do they drain my spirit?"*

The Right People Will Fuel Your Growth

When you're surrounded by the **right energy**, everything **feels easier**:

✓ **You feel inspired instead of doubtful.**

✓ **You take action instead of overthinking.**

✓ **You believe in your potential instead of questioning it.**

Example: Successful people surround themselves with **growth-minded individuals** because **iron sharpens iron.** If you're around motivated, positive, and goal-driven people, that energy will naturally push you higher.

Lesson? **Who you spend time with shapes who you become.** Choose relationships that align with your best self.

Protecting Your Energy is NOT Selfish

Many people feel guilty for **distancing themselves from toxic relationships** or prioritizing their own well-being. But the truth is:

✓ **You can't pour from an empty cup.**

✓ **Your peace is just as important as anyone else's.**

✓ **You owe it to yourself to create a life that feels GOOD to live.**

Mindset Shift: Instead of thinking, *"I don't want to hurt their feelings,"* remind yourself, *"I deserve to protect my peace and happiness."*

5. Being Alone is Okay, Too

One of the most powerful ways to **protect your energy** is by embracing **solitude.** In a world that constantly pushes social interaction, being alone is often misunderstood—but solitude isn't **loneliness**; it's **self-preservation.**

Sometimes, **the best thing you can do for yourself is to step back, take space, and recharge without external noise.**

Solitude is a Reset, Not a Problem

- **Being alone allows you to reflect** – Without outside influence, you can think clearly about what you want, need, and feel.
- **You realign with yourself** – Time alone helps you reconnect with your **own thoughts, dreams, and priorities.**

- **It helps you build emotional independence** – You stop relying on others for validation and become more self-assured.

Example: Have you ever felt mentally drained after **too much socializing**? That's your energy telling you to take a step back and reset.

Lesson? It's okay to unplug and take a break from people—it's actually healthy.

Don't Force Connections Just to Avoid Being Alone

Many people stay in **unfulfilling friendships or relationships** just because they're afraid of being alone. But the truth is:

Forcing connections that don't feel right drains you more than solitude ever will.

Being around the wrong energy is lonelier than being by yourself.

If you have to shrink yourself to fit in, it's not your space.

Mindset Shift: Instead of thinking, *"I don't want to be alone,"* remind yourself, *"I'd rather be alone than in the wrong company."*

The Strongest People Are Comfortable in Their Own Presence

Many assume that **constantly being surrounded by people** is a sign of strength. But in reality, **true strength comes from being secure in your own presence.**

- **You trust yourself more.**
- **You stop seeking external validation.**

- **You attract better connections because you're whole on your own.**

Example: The most successful, self-aware people **spend intentional time alone**—not because they don't enjoy company, but because they understand the **power of their own energy.**

6. Final Takeaway: Your Energy is Sacred

Your **energy is powerful, valuable, and sacred**—and the world **benefits from your light.** But if you're not careful, the wrong people, places, and habits can **dim that light** before you even realize it.

You are in control of who and what gets access to your energy.

Protecting Your Energy is Protecting Your Power

✓ **Prioritize spaces, people, and activities that uplift you.** If it doesn't bring you peace, joy, or growth, it's not worth your energy.

✓ **Set boundaries unapologetically.** Your well-being comes first— anyone who respects you will also respect your limits.

✓ **Listen to your intuition.** If something feels draining, misaligned, or toxic, trust yourself enough to step away.

Example: If a conversation, event, or relationship **consistently leaves you exhausted, anxious, or unmotivated,** that's your sign— it's not for you. Choose spaces that make you **feel strong, supported, and at peace.**

You Don't Owe Your Energy to Anyone Who Doesn't Respect It

You don't have to entertain draining conversations.

You don't have to explain your boundaries.

You don't have to be accessible to everyone, all the time.

Mindset Shift: Instead of feeling guilty for protecting your peace, remind yourself: *"My energy is mine to give, and I choose to give it where it's valued."*

Your energy shapes your reality. The more you protect it, the brighter your light shines—and the more you attract the right people, opportunities, and experiences into your life.

Reflection Exercise: Protecting Your Energy

Take a few moments to reflect on how you're managing your energy and where you might need to set stronger boundaries.

a. Energy Audit: Who & What Deserves Your Energy?

List **three people, places, or activities** that **energize you** and make you feel uplifted.

List **three people, places, or activities** that **drain you** and leave you feeling exhausted or unmotivated.

What patterns do you notice? What can you do to spend more time in energizing spaces and less in draining ones?

b. Identifying Your Energy Leaks

Think about the last **three times you felt mentally or emotionally drained.**

✓ What triggered that feeling?

✓ Was it a person, an environment, or a situation?

✓ Could you have set a boundary to protect your energy?

What changes can you make to prevent those energy drains in the future?

c. Setting Boundaries with Confidence

Write down **one area of your life** where you need **stronger boundaries** (work, relationships, social life, social media, etc.). Write a boundary statement that affirms your right to protect your peace.

Example:

✓ **Boundary:** *I will no longer entertain conversations that drain me or bring unnecessary negativity into my space.*

✓ **Action Step:** *The next time someone brings drama into my life, I will politely disengage or redirect the conversation.*

d. Recharging Your Energy

Write down **three activities that make you feel recharged, inspired, or at peace.**

Commit to doing at least **one of these activities this week** to refuel your energy.

Example:

✓ Spending time in nature

✓ Journaling or meditating

✓ Listening to uplifting music or a podcast

Your energy is sacred—be intentional about where it goes. The more you prioritize yourself, the more aligned, peaceful, and empowered you become.

Chapter 27: God at the Center – The Faith That Guides Me

For me, **God is everything**. He is at the **center of my life**, woven into every **thought, decision, and moment**. He is my **foundation, my protector, and my source of peace and wisdom**. No matter what I face—**joy, hardship, or uncertainty**—I know I am **never alone** because He is **always with me**.

This chapter is **personal**. It's about my **faith**, my **relationship with God**, and how **trusting in Him has shaped my life** in ways nothing else could. But I also recognize that **faith looks different for everyone**.

Some find their **guidance in God**. Some in **Allah**. Some in **the universe**. Some in a **deeper spiritual connection beyond a name. No matter what faith looks like to you, the power of believing in something greater than yourself is undeniable.**

Faith **isn't just about religion**—it's about having **a foundation that keeps you steady when life is uncertain. It's about having something to turn to when you don't have all the answers.**

1. Why Faith is Essential

Faith is more than just **believing**—it's **trusting**. It's the deep, unwavering knowing that even when things don't go as planned, even when life feels uncertain, **everything is working for a greater purpose.**

Faith isn't about **having all the answers**—it's about knowing that **you don't have to.** It's about believing that, even in the hardest moments, **you are never alone, never forgotten, and never without guidance.**

A heart with fear is a heart without God. When you truly trust in Him, fear no longer has control over you. Worry fades when you realize that **God is always in control, even when life feels chaotic.**

Why Faith is So Important

✓ **It gives you peace in the face of uncertainty.**

Life will always have ups and downs, but faith gives you **calmness in the storm**—a deep sense that, no matter what happens, you are being led toward something greater.

✓ **It reminds you that you are guided and supported at all times.**

Faith is knowing that you are never **walking this journey alone**—that there is a higher power leading you, protecting you, and surrounding you with love.

✓ **It helps you trust that good is always on its way.**

Even when things seem to be falling apart, faith reminds you that **they might actually be falling into place.**

My Personal Connection to Faith

For me, **God's presence is constant.** He is not just someone I turn to when I **need help**—He is in my **daily life, guiding me every step of the way.**

✓ **When I feel lost, I talk to Him.** He gives me clarity.

✓ **When I feel grateful, I thank Him.** He reminds me how blessed I am.

✓ **When I feel afraid, I lean on Him.** He strengthens me.

I don't see God as distant—I see Him as **my guide, my protector, and my strength.** Knowing He is on my side gives me **an unshakable sense of peace, no matter what life throws my way.**

Because **a heart with fear is a heart without God,** I choose faith over fear every time.

2. Faith and Expecting Good Things to Happen

Faith isn't just about **believing in God**—it's about believing that **good things are on their way to you.** It's about walking through life with an **expectation** that things are working in your favor, even when you can't see it yet.

Faith is Walking with Expectation

When you truly **trust in God,** you move differently. You walk with confidence, not fear. You trust that:

✓ **Things will work out.** Even when the road is unclear, you know there's a greater plan.

✓ **Every challenge has a lesson and a blessing.** Nothing happens by accident—everything is shaping you for what's next.

✓ **Even when things don't make sense now, they will later.** The pieces will always come together in time.

Example: Have you ever been through a difficult situation, only to look back later and realize **it led you to something even better?** That's faith in action—trusting that God's timing is always perfect.

Faith and the Law of Attraction: The Power of Expectation

Some call it **the law of attraction**—the idea that **what you believe and expect, you attract into your life.** But at its core, this is **also faith.**

When you trust that God is working things out for you, you are naturally attracting that goodness into your life.

✓ If you expect **problems and disappointments**, that's what you'll notice.

✓ If you expect **blessings and opportunities**, you'll start seeing them everywhere.

Mindset Shift: Instead of thinking *"What if things go wrong?"* shift to *"What if everything goes right?"*

Faith is Trusting in the Bigger Picture

Faith isn't just a belief—it's a **way of thinking, a way of living, a way of seeing the world.**

✓ Faith is expecting things to go right, not wrong.

✓ Faith is believing that even setbacks are setting you up for something better.

✓ Faith is trusting that your path is unfolding exactly as it should.

Example: When you **fully trust God**, you stop stressing over every detail. You don't need to **micromanage your blessings**—you just stay aligned, do your part, and **let Him handle the rest.**

What You Believe, You Receive

Whether you call it **faith, trust, or energy alignment**, the principle is the same:

What you believe, you receive. Expect blessings. Expect breakthroughs. Expect peace. Expect things to work out. Because when you trust in God, you'll always find yourself exactly where you need to be.

3. Surrendering to God's Plan

One of the **hardest but most freeing** things I've learned is to **let go and trust**.

For so long, I tried to **control everything**—to **force outcomes, stress about timing, and feel anxious when things weren't happening fast enough**. But the deeper my faith grew, the more I realized:

Trusting in God means surrendering that control.

Surrender **doesn't mean giving up**—it means knowing that **I don't have to have all the answers, because He does.**

What It Means to Surrender to God

✓ **It means releasing anxiety about the future.** When you trust in God's plan, you stop **overthinking every step** and start moving with **peace**.

✓ **It means shifting from control to faith.** Instead of **forcing things to happen**, you allow them to unfold in **divine timing**.

✓ **It means trusting that setbacks are setups.** If something doesn't work out, it's because **God has something better ahead.**

Example: Have you ever looked back on something you desperately wanted, only to realize later that **God was protecting you from it or preparing you for something greater?** That's the power of surrender.

How to Practice Surrender

Faith isn't just about believing—it's about **actively trusting and releasing control.** Here's how to do it daily:

✓ **When something is out of your control, pray instead of worrying.**

Instead of asking, *"What should I do?"*, say, *"God, I trust You to guide me."* Let go of the **need to figure it all out** on your own.

✓ **Replace "Why is this happening to me?" with "What is this teaching me?"**

Every challenge carries a **lesson** and a **blessing.** When you shift your perspective, you stop feeling like a **victim** and start seeing **growth.**

✓ **Trust that if something doesn't work out, something better is coming.**

Disappointments are often **redirections.** If a door closes, it's because **God has a greater one waiting for you.**

Mindset Shift: Instead of thinking, *"I need to make this happen now,"* say, *"I trust that what's meant for me will come in the right time."*

The Peace That Comes With Surrender

Surrendering to God's plan has given me the **greatest peace** in my life. I no longer feel the need to **fight against what is.** Instead, I trust that **everything—everything—is happening for my highest good, even when I don't understand it in the moment.**

Let go. Trust. Know that God's plan is bigger, better, and greater than anything you could have imagined.

4. Faith in Action – Walking with God Daily

Faith **isn't just a feeling**—it's an **everyday practice**, a way of life. **I walk with God in everything I do.** I talk to Him, I listen for His guidance, and I thank Him **even when I don't have what I want yet**—because I trust that **His timing is always perfect.**

For me, **God isn't just my protector—He's my best friend.**

Ways I Keep God at the Center of My Life
- **Prayer:** Talking to Him like a friend, not just when I need something but in **every moment.** Whether I'm grateful, struggling, or just thinking, I bring it to Him.
- **Gratitude:** Thanking Him for everything—**big and small**—because gratitude strengthens faith. **When you focus on what's good, you attract more blessings.**
- **Listening:** Paying attention to **signs, intuition, and the lessons He places in front of me.** Faith isn't just speaking—it's also about being still and listening.
- **Surrender:** Trusting that **He is leading me, even when I don't know the destination yet.** I no longer try to force things—I just follow where He guides me.

Faith Changes How You Move Through Life
When you walk in faith, **you move differently**:
- **You are no longer afraid of what's ahead.** You know you're being led.
- **You don't stress over what you can't control.** You trust that **God's got it.**

- **You find peace in uncertainty.** You stop forcing and start flowing.

Mindset Shift: Instead of saying, *"I hope things work out,"* start saying, *"I KNOW God is working things out for me."*

Faith is Trusting the Journey

Faith isn't just about **waiting for miracles**—it's about **walking with God daily**, trusting Him, leaning on Him, and knowing that He is **always beside you, leading the way.**

When you let God guide you, you don't have to fear what's next—because you KNOW you're being led to something greater.

5. Everyone's Faith is Unique

This is **my experience**, my **deep personal connection with God**. He is the center of my life, my guide, my best friend. But I also recognize that **faith is personal**—it looks different for everyone.

Some people find faith in **God/Allah, Buddha, or divine teachings.**
Some believe in **the universe, energy, or spiritual connection.**
Some trust in **their higher self, intuition, or inner wisdom.**

And that's okay. **Faith isn't about labels—it's about connection.**

What Truly Matters is Having Something to Believe In

It doesn't matter **what name you give it**—what matters is having **something that keeps you grounded, hopeful, and aligned.**
✓ **Something that gives you strength when life gets hard.**

✓ Something that reminds you that you're not alone.

✓ Something that helps you trust the process, even when it's unclear.

Example: Whether you call it **God, the universe, destiny, or divine timing,** the core belief remains the same—**that you are being guided, that things happen for a reason, and that you are always supported.**

At the End of the Day, Faith is About Trust

✓ **It's about trusting that you are exactly where you need to be.**

✓ **It's about believing that even challenges serve a purpose.**

✓ **It's about knowing you are being guided toward something greater, even when you can't see it yet.**

Mindset Shift: Instead of worrying about **what's next,** start trusting that **what's next is already being prepared for you.**

Faith is Knowing You Are Supported

No matter what name you give it, **faith is about trust.** It's about knowing that **you are never alone, never forgotten, and never without guidance.**

Faith isn't just believing in something greater—it's knowing that something greater believes in YOU.

6. Faith, Karma, and the Energy You Put Into the World

Faith isn't just about **trusting in God's plan**—it's also about understanding that **our actions have consequences.** Every thought we think, every word we speak, and every action we take **sends energy into the world**—and that energy **always finds its way back to us.**

This is the essence of **karma**—the idea that **what we give is what we receive.**

The Energy You Put Out Shapes Your Reality

✓ **Good energy brings good things.**

When you move with **kindness, love, and integrity**, life rewards you in ways you might not even realize. Unexpected blessings, aligned opportunities, and deeper peace come from **living with good intentions.**

✓ **Negative energy attracts challenges.**

If you act with **dishonesty, selfishness, or negativity**, those same energies tend to **find their way back to you.** Struggles, conflicts, and obstacles often reflect what we've put into the world.

Example: If you constantly move with jealousy and resentment, you'll always feel stuck. But if you move with **gratitude and faith**, you'll start to see more reasons to be thankful.

Karma, Faith, and Divine Balance

Some people see **karma** as **God's way of balancing things out.** Others see it as **the universe responding to the energy we create.** No matter how you frame it, the message remains the same:

✓ **What you put out into the world, you get back.**

✓ **Your energy, intentions, and actions shape your experiences.**

✓ **You are always creating your reality through the way you show up in life.**

Mindset Shift: Instead of asking, *"Why is this happening to me?"* ask yourself, *"What energy am I putting out, and how can I shift it?"*

Living with Intention and Integrity

When you live with **faith and positive energy**, you naturally attract **better things** into your life:

✔ **Move with love, and you'll receive more love.**

✔ **Give without expectation, and blessings will come unexpectedly.**

✔ **Stay honest and authentic, and the right people will find you.**

Final Reminder: **God, the universe, or destiny—whatever you believe in—is always watching. Live with intention, integrity, and faith, and life will reflect that energy back to you.**

What You Give is What You Receive

Faith isn't just about believing—it's about aligning your energy with the life you want to create.

Put out love, and love returns. Move with faith, and faith rewards you. Stay true to your values, and life will meet you with blessings.

Reflection Exercise: Strengthening Your Faith

Take a moment to reflect on **how faith has shown up in your life** and how you can strengthen it moving forward.

1. Remembering a Time Faith Worked for You

Think of a time when something worked out for you, even when you doubted it would.

- What happened?
- How did it teach you to trust more?

Example: Maybe you were worried about a financial situation, but the right opportunity showed up just in time. Maybe you were heartbroken over something that didn't work out, only to realize later that it was a blessing in disguise.

What did that experience teach you about trusting the process?

2. Trusting What's Meant for You

Write down three things you are trusting will happen in your life.

These could be **dreams, goals, relationships, healing, or breakthroughs** you desire.

Instead of worrying about **how** they will happen, affirm: *I trust that this is already being worked out for me.*

Example:

✓ *I trust that I am being guided to the right career opportunities.*

✓ *I trust that my relationships will align with love and peace.*

✓ *I trust that my health, happiness, and success are unfolding in divine timing.*

Let go of the need to control the outcome and trust that it is already in motion.

3. Expressing Gratitude for Divine Guidance

If you believe in **God, the universe, or a higher power**, take a moment to **express gratitude.**

Say this out loud or write it down:

"Thank you for always guiding me, even when I can't see the full picture."

✓ **Gratitude strengthens faith**—it reminds you that you are always supported, always protected, and never alone.

Trust the Journey

Faith is knowing that even when you can't see the path, it's still leading you somewhere great.

Keep trusting, keep believing, and know that everything is unfolding exactly as it should.

Practicing Good Karma in Your Daily Life

If you want to **attract more positivity** into your life, start by being **intentional about the energy you put out.** The energy you send into the world always **finds its way back to you**—whether through opportunities, relationships, or unexpected blessings.

Good karma isn't about **seeking rewards**—it's about creating a world where **love, kindness, and goodness multiply.** And when you live with **faith and integrity**, you walk through life with **peace**, knowing that everything is unfolding **exactly as it should.**

Ways to Put Out Positive Energy Daily

✓ **Be Kind, Even When No One's Watching.**

The energy of kindness **never goes to waste**. A small act—holding the door, giving a compliment, or offering a helping hand—can **create a ripple effect of positivity.**

✓ **Forgive and Release.**

Holding onto grudges **only brings negativity** into your own heart. Letting go doesn't mean excusing someone's behavior—it means **freeing yourself from the weight of resentment** so you can make space for **better things.**

✓ **Give Without Expectation.**

True generosity comes from **a place of abundance, not obligation.** Whether it's time, love, or resources, giving freely **always returns to you in some form**—sometimes in ways you never expected.

✓ **Choose Honesty and Integrity.**

Being truthful and honorable in your actions **creates a foundation of trust, peace, and self-respect.** Even when no one is watching, **you know you're doing the right thing.**

Final Thought: Karma, Faith, and Inner Peace

When you move with **good intentions, trust, and kindness**, you don't have to worry about **what's coming next.**

What you give, you receive.

What you put into the world, you get back.

When you align your actions with goodness, life aligns with you.

Keep walking in faith, keep putting out positive energy, and watch how life rewards you in ways greater than you ever imagined.

Conclusion: Listening Within – The Journey That Changes Everything

You've made it this far, which means you're already taking the most important step: **listening—not just to the world around you, but to yourself.**

That's no small feat in an **overstimulated, fast-moving world** that constantly demands your attention, pulling you in a hundred different directions. But here you are—**choosing awareness, choosing growth, choosing YOU.**

Through this book, we've explored **understanding, balance, self-awareness, and growth.** Along the way, you've discovered:

✓ **Active listening deepens your connection**—not just with others, but with yourself.

✓ **Perspective and neutrality bring clarity and peace**—allowing you to navigate life with wisdom instead of reaction.

✓ **Your "why" is your anchor**—keeping you grounded, no matter how strong the storm.

✓ **Positivity is a choice**—and happiness isn't something you wait for, it's something you create **every single day.**

But the biggest takeaway of all?

The journey always starts within.

Everything you seek—**peace, fulfillment, purpose, alignment—starts with you.** The more you nurture your **mind, soul, and energy**, the more your outer world reflects that inner strength.

Now, as we close this chapter, let's talk about **what it truly means to carry these lessons forward—to not just understand them, but to live them.** Because the real journey? **It begins now.**

The World is Yours to Shape

Everything you do—**every choice you make, every step you take**—reflects what's happening inside of you.

The way you see the world is directly influenced by the way you see **yourself.** Your mindset, your energy, and your beliefs **shape your reality**—and the good news is, you have the power to **shift, grow, and create the life you truly want.**

The Inner World Shapes the Outer World

✓ **When you nurture your inner world, your outer world shifts in response.**

Your experiences, relationships, and opportunities change **when you change.**

✓ **When you create peace within, you start seeing more peace outside of you.**

A calm mind leads to a calm approach to life. You stop reacting to chaos and start **choosing clarity.**

✓ **When you listen to yourself, your decisions become clearer, more intentional, and aligned with who you truly are.**

No more second-guessing, no more living for outside validation— just **full alignment with your truth.**

Example: How Your Mindset Shapes Your Reality

If you focus on gratitude, growth, and positivity... Your experience of life will feel **richer, more fulfilling, and full of possibility.**

If you let yourself be consumed by fear, self-doubt, or negativity... The world will feel **heavy, stressful, and closed off**—even when good things are happening around you.

Progress Over Perfection

✓ **Your reality is a reflection of your mindset, your beliefs, and your choices.**

✓ **This isn't about being perfect—it's about being intentional.**

✓ **It's about making small, conscious decisions every day.**

    Choosing to listen.

    Choosing to grow.

    Choosing to show up as your most authentic self.

    The world is **yours to shape**—and it all begins **within.**

You Already Have Everything You Need

The answers you've been searching for **aren't out there**—they've been inside you all along.

We often look **outside of ourselves** for validation, direction, or reassurance, but the truth is:

✓ **You don't need permission to trust yourself.**

✓ **You don't need external validation to know your worth.**

✓ **You don't need to have all the answers right now—just the willingness to listen to yourself and move forward.**

Everything you need to **thrive, grow, and succeed is already within you.**

Example: Your Inner Voice Always Knows

Think back to times when you've felt **lost, anxious, or unsure.**

✓ What has always guided you back to clarity?

✓ Was it someone else's opinion? External noise?

✓ Or was it something **deeper**—your own **inner voice** reminding you of what truly matters?

The truth is, **your intuition, your wisdom, and your experience have always been guiding you.** When you quiet the outside noise and truly listen, **you already know what you need.**

The Power of Self-Trust

✓ **By honoring your needs, trusting your intuition, and building self-awareness, you'll find the clarity and strength you've been looking for.**

✓ **The more you trust yourself, the more life aligns in your favor.**

✓ **You are already enough. You already have what it takes.**

The world may offer guidance, but the real answers? They've always been within you.

Your Next Step

As you close this book, **remember: this is just the beginning.**

Reading and learning are powerful, but **true transformation happens when you apply what you've gained.**

✓ **Knowledge is only powerful when you apply it.**

✓ **Insights only change your life when you act on them.**

So... **what now?**

How to Take This Journey Forward
Put the tools and lessons into practice.

Change doesn't happen overnight, but small, intentional steps **lead to big transformations.**

Listen to yourself first.

Before making a decision, pause and ask:
"What do I truly feel? What do I truly need?"

Build your foundation.

Take time to:
- **Understand yourself.**
- **Set boundaries.**
- **Prioritize what makes you feel fulfilled.**

Fuel yourself with your "why."

On the hard days, let your purpose guide you forward. When things get tough, **remind yourself why you started.**

Choose happiness every day.

Even when life isn't perfect, **there is always something to be grateful for.** Focus on that.

It's About Progress, Not Perfection

You don't have to change everything all at once. **Growth is a daily choice.**

✓ **Every day, choose to be a little more intentional.**

✓ **Every day, choose to be a little more present.**

✓ Every day, choose to be a little more aligned with yourself.
This is your journey. **Trust it. Own it. And step into the life that was meant for you.**

You're Not Alone on This Journey

No matter where you are in life, **you are not alone.**

✓ **Everyone you meet is navigating their own path.**

✓ **Everyone has struggles, fears, and uncertainties—just like you.**

✓ **Everyone is learning, growing, and figuring things out, one step at a time.**

The difference? **Some people choose to do it with awareness, compassion, and balance.** And when you make that choice, you **not only transform your own life, but you inspire others to do the same.**

The Power of How You Show Up

When you show up as your most authentic self...
You create space for others to do the same.

When you listen without judgment...
You encourage deeper, more meaningful connections.

When you operate from a place of clarity and self-trust...
You give others permission to trust themselves, too.

The way you live, the energy you bring, and the choices you make **don't just affect you—they ripple out into the world.**

Be the Light the World Needs

✓ By living with awareness, you become a light in a world that needs more of it.

✓ By choosing growth, you encourage others to grow, too.

✓ By trusting yourself, you remind others that they can trust themselves as well.

This journey isn't just personal—it's collective. And the more you step into your truth, the more you inspire others to do the same.

Closing Thought

This is your **world.**

This is your **journey.**

This is your **time.**

✓ **Embrace it fully.**

✓ **Live it authentically.**

✓ **And never stop listening within.**

Everything you need is already inside of you. **Trust yourself. Trust your path. And step into the life that was always meant for you.**

Acknowledgments

This book would not have been possible without the experiences, lessons, and even challenges that shaped my understanding of life.

To everyone who ever shared wisdom with me, asked the right questions, or made me think differently—thank you.

To my friends and family—your support, love, and patience mean everything to me.

To my readers—thank you for being on this journey with me. My hope is that this book gives you the clarity, confidence, and purpose you deserve.

And lastly, to my past self—thank you for never settling, never stopping, and always striving for more. This one's for you.

Author Bio

Bridgette Gajadhar is a writer, truth-seeker, and modern-day philosopher known for turning real life into real talk. Her work bridges the gap between clarity and action—pushing readers to think deeply, live honestly, and show up with intention. She's the founder of Pons Veritas, a platform dedicated to helping people reconnect with who they really are, what they truly want, and how to live a life that reflects both.

Born with a sharp mind and a soft heart, Bridgette's approach to personal growth is raw, empowering, and refreshingly unfiltered. She doesn't believe in fluff or performative positivity—only the kind of self-awareness that actually leads to change. Whether she's writing about purpose, ego, self-love, communication, or resilience, every word comes from lived experience and unshakable insight.

Bridgette's style is both relatable and revolutionary. She speaks to the overthinkers, the go-getters, the ones who feel everything deeply and still keep pushing forward. Her books don't just talk about healing and growth—they show you how to live it, day by day, moment by moment.

The Inner Clarity & Self-Mastery series is designed to help you stop settling and start living with intention. It's not about having all the answers—it's about finally asking the right questions.

To stay connected, visit www.ponsveritas.com and subscribe for updates, new releases, exclusive downloads, and a steady dose of truth you won't find anywhere else.

www.ingramcontent.com/pod-product-compliance
Lightning Source LLC
Chambersburg PA
CBHW071703120626
46550CB00001B/87